Reading About Biology

Edited by Steuart Kellington

**Nigel Green
Steuart Kellington
Wilf Stout**

Heinemann Educational Books

Heinemann Educational Books
22 Bedford Square, London WC1B 3HH

LONDON EDINBURGH MELBOURNE AUCKLAND SINGAPORE
KUALA LUMPUR NEW DELHI IBADAN NAIROBI JOHANNESBURG
PORTSMOUTH (NH) KINGSTON

ISBN 0 435 57522 8

The publishers wish to thank the following for permission to reproduce photographs: All Sport 15.3; Heather Angel/Biofotos 17.4, 20.1, 25.1, 27.2; Barnaby's Picture Library 10.1; BBC Copyright 3.1; Biofoto Associates 3.4(a)(b), 4.1(a)(b), 4.3(a)(b), 6.1, 6.3, 8.1, 9.1, 9.3, 26.1; Blacks of Greenock 16.2; C. Carvalho, Frank Lane Agency 17.2; J. Allan Cash 20.3, 28.1; Dr J. A. L. Cooke, Oxford Scientific Films 5.1; Eric Crichton, Bruce Coleman 7.3; The Daily Telegraph 20.4; Peter David, Planet Earth Pictures 26.2, 26.3; Tim Graham 23.1; Frants Hartmann, Frank Lane Agency 17.3; H. J. Heinz 7.4; ICL 18.1; Jaguar Cars 18.4, 22.3, 22.4, 22.5; Massey Ferguson 22.8; Norman Myers, Bruce Coleman 2.1; Oxfam 28.2, 28.3; Plant Breeding Institute, Cambridge 24.1; Betty Rawlings Photo Service 2.2, 3.3, 8.4(1)(2), 30.3; Rolls Royce Cars 22.7; Lee Rue, Frank Lane Agency 16.3; Safeway Food Stores 7.1; Science Photo Library 11.3, 19.3, 21.3; Sport and General 14.1; Sporting Pictures (UK) 13.1, 13.3, 15.1, 15.2, 15.4; Irene Vandermolen, Frank Lane Agency 16.4; R. S. Virdee, Frank Lane Agency 5.2; WHO (World Health Organisation) 30.1.

Typeset in 11/12pt Photina by
BAS Printers Limited, Over Wallop, Hampshire

Printed and bound in Great Britain by
Scotprint Ltd, Musselburgh

Contents

1 Photosynthesis

Plants make food from carbon dioxide gas and water using a process called **photosynthesis**. Energy from sunlight is also needed for photosynthesis. The process takes place in the green substance **chlorophyll** which is found in all living plants. Food made by photosynthesis is used by plants to build new cells, to repair old cells, to move substances around the plant and to provide food stores.

Photosynthesis is affected by many different factors. We shall be looking at one of the most important of these—light intensity.

The factory in a leaf

Photosynthesis takes place mainly in the leaves of a plant. Fig. 1 shows a narrow slice of a section through a leaf. Work down the diagram from the top to understand the main parts of a leaf. Then look at the 'cutaway diagram' [Fig. 2] of a **chloroplast**. Follow the numbers 1 to 4 to see the chemical changes which take place.

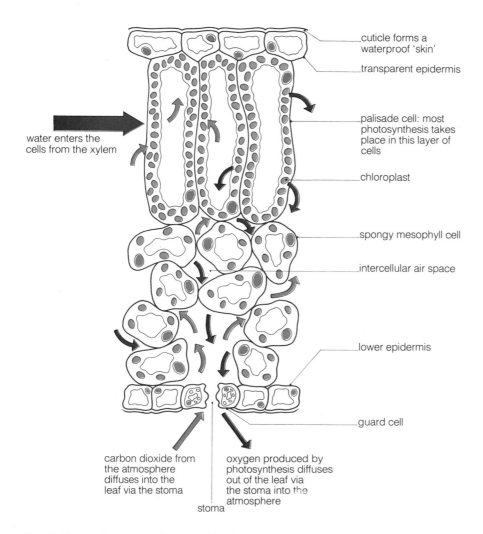

cuticle forms a waterproof 'skin'

transparent epidermis

palisade cell: most photosynthesis takes place in this layer of cells

chloroplast

water enters the cells from the xylem

spongy mesophyll cell

intercellular air space

lower epidermis

guard cell

carbon dioxide from the atmosphere diffuses into the leaf via the stoma

oxygen produced by photosynthesis diffuses out of the leaf via the stoma into the atmosphere

stoma

Fig. 1 Vertical section of a typical leaf

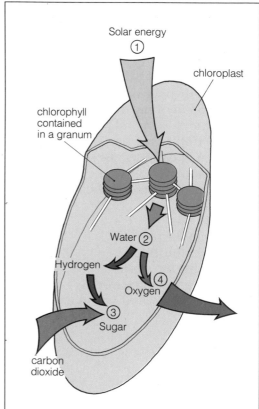

Solar energy ①

chloroplast

chlorophyll contained in a granum

Water ②

Hydrogen

Oxygen ④

Sugar ③

carbon dioxide

Fig. 2 Cutaway section of a chloroplast

1 Light reaction Light energy from the sun is absorbed by chlorophyll in the chloroplasts.

2 The light energy is used to split molecules of water into hydrogen and oxygen molecules.

3 Dark reaction Hydrogen gas combines with carbon dioxide gas to form sugar.

4 During the day, oxygen not used in respiration leaves the plant through the stomata.

Photosynthesis and light intensity

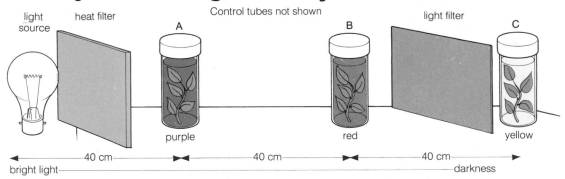

Look at Fig. 3 showing three sealed glass tubes. The tubes are in a darkened room and are placed at different distances from a lamp. Each tube contains hydrogencarbonate indicator, and they all start the same colour as the control. This indicator changes colour from yellow to red to purple as the concentration of carbon dioxide in the tubes decreases. In this way, the colour of the indicator shows how the concentration of carbon dioxide is changing.

A sheet of glass is placed between the lamp and the tubes. This glass is labelled 'heat filter' in the diagram. The lamp is switched on and the experiment is left for several hours. The indicator in each tube is then examined for a change in colour. Fig. 3 shows some typical results.

How plants adapt to different light conditions

Trees need to collect sunlight to produce food. In shady areas, trees arrange their leaves so that they overlap as little as possible. This arrangement gives the greatest leaf area to catch sunlight.

Even leaves on the same tree vary in size and shape according to their position. For example, on one tree, the leaves growing in a shaded area are thinner and let through more light than leaves growing in a sunny position.

Like all organisms, plants break down food by respiration to release energy for growth. Therefore, plants must receive sufficient light for a long enough period to replace the food which has been used. When respiration and photosynthesis are taking place at the same rate (e.g. during early morning) there is no net gain or loss of food, and the plant is said to be at its **compensation point**. Plants adapted to living in the shade reach their compensation point more quickly than plants living in bright sunlight [Fig. 4]. This enables them to begin replacing their food reserves much earlier in the day than the other plants and therefore for a longer period of time. This makes up for their slower rate of photosynthesis when in light of low intensity.

Fig. 3 The results of an experiment investigating the effects of light intensity on the rate of photosynthesis in pondweed. The same experiment was set up with control tubes (not shown) containing only indicator.

A High rate of photosynthesis
B Slower rate of photosynthesis
C Respiration faster than photosynthesis

Control No change in colour. This indicates that the changes in colour in the experimental tubes were the results of the reaction occurring in the pondweed.

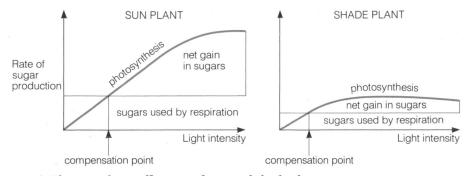

Fig. 4 Photosynthetic efficiency of sun and shade plants

2 How do plants drink?

Fig. 1 A giant redwood

Fig. 2 A greenhouse in early morning

Look at the photograph of the huge redwood tree [Fig. 1]. The redwood is able to 'pump' water 70 metres up to its highest branches. An oak tree 'drinks' more than 2000 litres per day! How are these water supplies provided? A large block of flats usually has an electrical water pump to force water to a supply tank at the top. But trees obtain sufficient water without using electricity.

In this chapter we think about two processes going on in trees which help them to obtain water. These are called **transpiration** and **root pressure**. Both make use of **osmosis**, a process in which water diffuses through membranes from weaker to stronger solutions. Transpiration involves a force which 'pulls' water up the tree. Root pressure involves a force which 'pushes' water up the tree.

Drinking by 'pulling'

Look at the photograph of the greenhouse taken one morning [Fig. 2]. The windows have misted up with droplets of water. This is caused by plants losing water vapour by evaporation through millions of tiny pores in their leaves called **stomata** (plural of stoma). The water vapour then condenses on the cold greenhouse glass. This loss of water vapour via the stomata of plants is called **transpiration**.

Now look at the diagram of a leaf in *1 Photosynthesis*. The water vapour lost from the stomata comes from the spongy mesophyll cells just above the lower epidermis. As these cells lose water, their cell sap becomes more concentrated, so water passes to them from neighbouring cells by osmosis. As these neighbouring cells lose water their cell sap becomes more concentrated so their neighbouring cells supply water to them, and so on. Eventually water is drawn from the **xylem**. This is the tissue in leaves which carries the main water supply.

The xylem is a system of minute tubes reaching from the tips of the roots of the tree to each leaf [Fig. 3]. You can think of the xylem as being like the pipes of the water supply reaching from a reservoir to each house in a town.

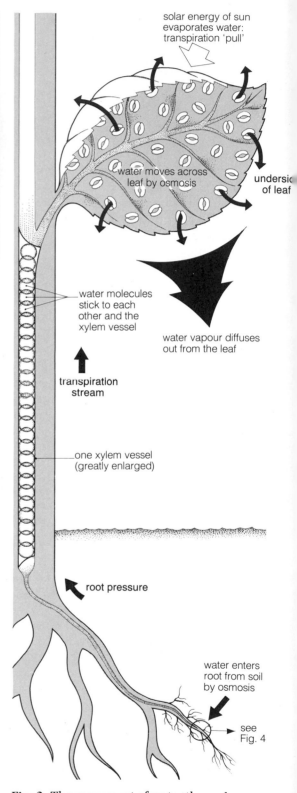

solar energy of sun
evaporates water:
transpiration 'pull'

water moves across
leaf by osmosis

undersi
of leaf

water vapour diffuses
out from the leaf

water molecules
stick to each
other and the
xylem vessel

transpiration
stream

one xylem vessel
(greatly enlarged)

root pressure

water enters
root from soil
by osmosis

see
Fig. 4

Fig. 3 The movement of water through a plant

The water in the xylem is continuous from the roots to the leaves and may be 70 metres long in a large tree. The long tubes of water, containing dissolved mineral salts, are held together through a strange property of water molecules. The molecules 'stick' to each other and also to the sides of the xylem tubes. So when water is lost from the leaves by transpiration, water molecules are pulled along the whole length of the xylem, even from as far away as the roots. (You can imagine the water in the xylem as a long thin piece of string. When the string is pulled at one end (in the leaves), the far end (in the roots) moves, even though it is a long way away).

Drinking by 'pushing'

Transpiration pulls water up the trunk of a tree from its roots, but how does water enter the roots? **Osmosis** provides the answer. The cells in the roots contain **sap**. As water is drawn from the root cells into the xylem of the root, the sap in the root cells becomes more concentrated. So water is drawn in from neighbouring cells. These cells, in turn, draw in water from their neighbours. Eventually, the cells forming the fine root hairs are involved [Fig. 4]. These cells have sap which is usually far more concentrated than the soil water solution around them. Osmosis then produces a 'sucking' effect to draw in water from the soil and 'push' water into the trunk for a short distance. This 'push' is called **root pressure**.

A pump with no moving parts

Root pressure causes water to be drawn in from the soil through osmosis. Transpiration then pulls up the water to each leaf. The system is very effective when you think about the giant redwood trees and oak trees! The system does not fail even when there is a power cut! But it will stop working if a 'ring' is cut around the bark of the tree through which water flows.

Why do plants drink anyway?

Here is a list of seven reasons for plants to take in water.

1 It acts as the liquid in which minerals and food materials dissolve. These soluble materials can be transported in solution to different parts of the plant.
2 During photosynthesis water combines with carbon dioxide in the presence of light energy and chlorophyll to form carbohydrates.
3 The carbohydrates formed in 2 are broken down in respiration, and energy is released to drive all other plant activities.
4 Combined with nitrogen, carbohydrates can be made into protein and used for growth and repair.
5 Water helps to regulate the temperature of the plant in hot conditions. When water is evaporated from the leaves, heat is lost from the plant. This helps to cool the leaves and prevent them from being scorched by the sun.
6 Water is essential for the germination of seeds.
7 Water enters the rapidly growing cells during root and shoot growth. It fills the cells and inflates them. This helps to keep the shape of the soft parts of the growing plant. In this way, young stems and leaves become erect and firm.

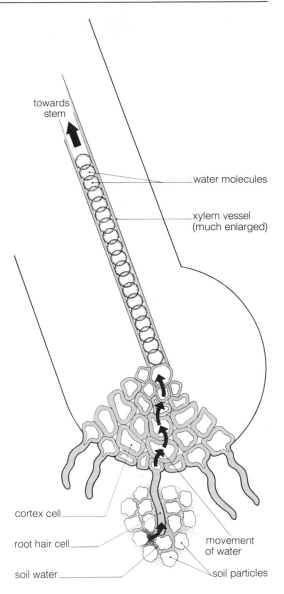

Fig. 4 The movement of water across a root

QUESTIONS

1 How does water reach the stomata from the leaf xylem during transpiration?
2 How is root pressure produced?
3 How many external factors can you think of that might affect the rate of water loss from a plant?
4 If the bark of trees is nibbled away by rabbits during winter, the trees usually die in the following spring. Why does this happen?
5 How do you think that dew is formed?

3 Do plants move?

Have you read *The Day of the Triffids* by John Wyndham? It is a science-fiction novel about plants which roam about the countryside killing people [Fig. 1]. We may laugh at such a thought because we all know that plants do not roam around. They are fixed to the ground by their roots. But plants do move. In common with every living organism, plants share the characteristic feature called **movement**.

Most animals move their whole bodies from place to place. (This is called **locomotion**.) Animals also move parts of their bodies. For example, you move your hands and eyes, sea anemones wave their tentacles and butterflies move their limbs, antennae and wings. Plants too can move parts of their plant bodies. For example, roots move down through the soil, stems move upwards and flower buds open.

Animals move from place to place to obtain food, to find a mate and to escape from their enemies. Plants do not need to move from place to place. They make their own food and they produce a new generation through self-pollination or by pollen moved by wind, insects or other animals. As plants cannot escape from their enemies, some have ways of avoiding damage by animals. These ways include the use of thorns, spines, prickles, poisons, nasty chemicals and others which you can read about below.

Fig. 1 Imagine being chased home at night by this!

Fig. 2 Seeing how pea plants grow

Stimulus and response

The ability of animals and plants to be sensitive to changes in their environment and respond to these changes is called **irritability**. This is another characteristic feature of all living organisms. Any change in the environment which can be detected by a living organism is called a **stimulus**. The change brought about in the organism is called a **response**. Because plants are fixed in one place, any movement in response to a stimulus can only be made by part of the plant.

Plants can make two kinds of movement as a response. If the response movement is due to stimulus from one direction only, the response is called **tropic** movement (tropism). If the movement is due to a stimulus from several or all directions, the response is called **nastic** movement.

You can now read about some tropic and nastic movements and how they occur.

Tropic movements

You may have grown peas in a jam jar like those in Fig. 2. Have you ever wondered why the roots always grow downwards and the shoots upwards? Parts of the plant make a response to the stimulus of gravity. This ability is called **geotropism**. It enables the roots to find water and the leaves to find light.

Have you noticed what happens to the leaves and stems of pot plants when placed on a window sill? They lean over towards the light [Fig. 3]. The movement is due to the stimulus of light and is called **phototropism**. ('Photo' is from the Greek word meaning 'light' and is also used in 'photograph'.) It enables the leaves to obtain more light for photosynthesis.

Fig. 3 Plants lean towards the light

Fig. 4 *Mimosa pudica* (**a**) before and (**b**) after being touched

(a)

(b)

The other important tropic movements are due to water and touch. The response due to water is called **hydrotropism**. The response due to touch is called **haptotropism**. When plants react to one of these stimuli they move by *growing* towards or away from the stimulus. Most of these growth responses are controlled by chemical substances produced by the plants. They act in a similar way to hormones in animals, but the responses occur much more slowly in plants than in animals.

Nastic movements

Sleep movements

Have you noticed that the petals of a daisy open in the early morning and close at nightfall? By closing at nightfall, the petals protect the inner parts of the flower from moisture.

Petals of the moonflower, evening primrose and the four o'clock plant open in the early evening and close in the early morning. Their petals work in the opposite way to daisy petals! Night-flowering plants need to keep their petals open at night because they are pollinated by insects which fly at night.

These responses of the petals are due to the stimulus of light. They are called **nastic** movements because the stimulus of light is not limited to a single direction. As with tropic movements, they are caused by the growth of cells. The petals of the daisy, for example, open in the morning because the cells on the inside surfaces grow faster than the cells on the outer surfaces of the petals. At nightfall, the petals close up because the cells on the outer surfaces grow faster than the cells on the inner surfaces.

Touch movements

The *Mimosa pudica* plant [Fig. 4] reacts dramatically to touch to give itself protection. It collapses immediately! But it can restore its shape within ten minutes. The mimosa has swellings at the base of each leaflet, leaf and leaf stalk. Each swelling contains cells with vacuoles full of water. But the cells are separated by large spaces. When part of the plant is touched, water is lost rapidly into the spaces between the cells and so that part collapses. This sudden change in the shape of the plant protects it from being damaged by whatever produced the stimulus.

QUESTIONS

1 Explain the difference between tropic and nastic movements.
2 Give a simple explanation in your own words of how a plant is able to 'move' towards light when placed on a windowsill.
3 Describe the movement of the petals of an evening primrose plant during a twenty-four hour period. Why do the petals move in this way?
4 A sprouting potato was left in the dark and another left in the light, for two weeks. After this time the shoots of the potato grown in the dark were observed to be longer than those of the potato grown in the light. Why was this?
5 Explain how tropic movements help plants to live successfully.

4 Looking into cells

It has taken over 400 years for scientists to be sure that all living things are made up of cells. And our understanding of cells has grown in step with the development of microscopes. As microscopes have improved, scientists have been able to probe deeper into cells to study their structure and how they work. In this chapter you can read about some important steps in our understanding of cells and how they are linked with microscopes.

The light microscope

The early years

In 1666 Robert Hooke, an Englishman, was observing thin slices of cork through a microscope. He saw that cork was made up of tiny box-like structures which he called **cells.**

Ten years later, a Dutchman called Anton Van Leeuwenhoek began to study plants and animals through microscopes. He also noticed that living material was made up of cells.

As the quality of microscopes improved, more details of living materials could be observed. In 1839, a Belgian botanist called Schleiden and a German zoologist called Schwann proposed the **cell theory**. This theory stated that all living things are made up of cells.

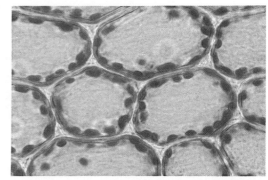

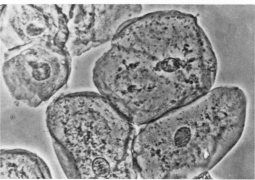

Fig. 1 (a) A plant cell (b) An animal cell

Fig. 2 Relative sizes of different cells

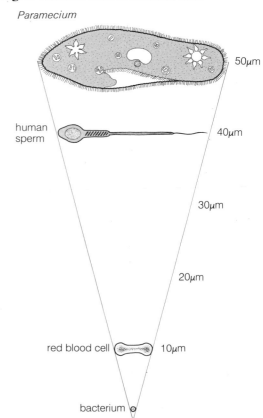

Using a light microscope

A modern light microscope can magnify objects up to 1500 times. But great care has to be taken in preparing specimens for observation. Specimens must be thin and transparent because light must pass through them before passing through the lenses. Very thin sections of plant and animal material are cut and stained and then placed on microscope slides. Look at the photographs of a plant cell and an animal cell as observed through a light microscope [Fig. 1 (a), (b)].

The basic structure of cells

Plant cells are surrounded by a **cell wall**. This is the outer covering found in all plant cells but absent from all animal cells. The cell wall is made from cellulose which is a non-living substance. Molecules can pass freely through a cell wall in either direction.

All cells have a **cell membrane**. In animal cells, the cell membrane is the outer covering of the cell. But in plant cells the cell membrane lies just inside the cell wall. The cell membrane is very thin and flexible and it holds the cell together. The membrane is made from protein and fats and it controls which substances can enter and leave the cell.

The bulk of a cell is made of **cytoplasm**. Under a light microscope, cytoplasm looks like jelly. Cytoplasm is made up of a mixture of carbohydrates, fats, proteins and water. To probe the cytoplasm further, a more powerful microscope than the light microscope is needed.

10

The electron microscope

Light microscopes enable scientists to study the form of cells and to understand some of the ways in which they work. But understanding of cells has grown rapidly since the *electron* microscope came into use about 40 years ago. A modern electron microscope can magnify up to 500 000 times. If a full stop on this page were magnified as much as this it would be larger than a tennis court!

There are no glass lenses in an electron microscope. Instead of light, a beam of electrons passes through the specimen before being focused by powerful magnets to give an image on a screen rather like a TV screen. Electrons are charged particles and move at high speed through the microscope. They can travel only very short distances through air and solids. So all the air has to be pumped out of the microscope and specimens must be very thin. There are many complicated parts in an electron microscope and it is very expensive to buy. It requires skilled technicians to operate electron microscopes and to prepare specimens.

Probing the cytoplasm

The cytoplasm looks like jelly through a light microscope. But when viewed through an electron microscope the cytoplasm is seen to be made up of vast numbers of tiny structures called **organelles**. ('Organelle' comes from a Latin word meaning 'small organ'. An organ is part of an animal or plant which carries out a special task like the liver or a stamen.) Organelles are bounded by membranes and are found in various shapes and sizes. Each organelle has a special task to carry out in the chemistry of a cell.

The sizes of cells and structures seen within cells are measured in units called *micrometres*. The abbreviation used for this measurement is μm. A micrometre is one-thousandth of a millimetre and there are one million micrometres to the metre. The sizes of various cells are shown in Fig. 2.

Chloroplasts

Look at the photograph in Fig. 3(a) of a plant cell taken through an electron microscope. You can see a **chloroplast**. This is a very important organelle in plant cells. Chloroplasts contain the green pigment **chlorophyll** which is used to absorb light energy for photosynthesis. You can read more about photosynthesis in *1 Photosynthesis*.

Nucleus

Look at Figs. 3(a) and (b), photographs of a plant cell and an animal cell taken through an electron microscope. Find the nucleus in each cell: it appears as a large spherical organelle. A nucleus contains chromosomes which are used by the cell to pass on information, for instance when the cell divides to make new cells. You can read more about chromosomes in *21 DNA and the genetic code*. The nucleus is a kind of 'brain' for a cell because it controls how it works and what it does.

Cells and microscopes

In this chapter you have read about cells and how our understanding of cells has grown over the years. A deep understanding of cells has been possible because of the improvements made in microscopes. Our understanding of most branches of science depends upon the apparatus which is available and the skills of the technicians who operate it.

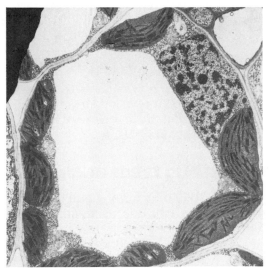
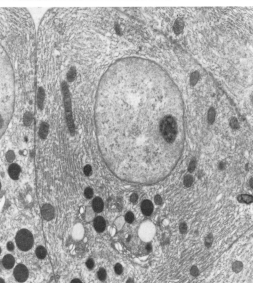

Fig. 3 (**a**) A plant cell (**b**) An animal cell

QUESTIONS

1 What does magnification mean?
2 How many similarities and differences between plant and animal cells can you think of?
3 If a plant cell and an animal cell are placed in distilled water, the animal cell swells up and bursts. However, the plant cell swells up a little, becomes rigid and does not burst. Why is this?
4 Read again the section on the **nucleus** of a cell. Use this and information in *21 DNA and the genetic code* to explain briefly how chromosomes pass on information to new cells.
5 Why has it taken so long to find out how cells work? Do you think that there is much more to learn?

5 Feeding on others

Plants make their own food by photosynthesis (see *1 Photosynthesis*). Animals cannot make their own food. They must gather food by eating plants or other animals.

A bed bug feeds again

It was 5.30 in the morning and John was fast asleep. He didn't know that he wasn't the only occupant of his bed. A bed bug was sharing it with him. The bug was feeling hungry as it hadn't eaten for weeks. Now was the time to enjoy its food—human blood!

The bug carefully probed John's skin to find a good spot to feed from. It inserted its needle-like tubular mouthparts through John's skin and penetrated one of his blood capillaries. If John had been awake it would have felt like a pin-prick. Normally, after his skin had been pricked a blood clot would quickly have stopped any bleeding. The bug had to prevent this process or the tubes in its mouthparts would have become blocked. The bug quickly pumped some saliva down one of its tubes into John's capillary. The saliva contained a chemical to stop the blood from clotting. The bug then sucked up a mixture of blood and saliva into its body.

It took the bug just twelve minutes to fill itself [Fig. 1]. In this time it had sucked up six times its body weight of blood. It left John sleeping soundly. The bug could last for up to a year on that meal—so John might not have to provide another meal for some time!

Fig. 1 A bed bug after a meal

The gnu and the lioness

It was dusk and the old gnu was feeding rapidly. Her sharp teeth quickly cut the African grass. Then she swallowed it straight down. The gnu had spotted a lioness eyeing her from a nearby acacia thicket. She had to eat lots of grass to give her the energy and goodness her body needed. The problem was that every time she began to eat she had to lower her eyes, and the noise of eating made it difficult to hear the sound around her. So she was constantly in danger of a sudden attack by the lioness. The gnu had always managed to escape before, but now she was old and slower.

Perfectly still, the lioness watched the gnu grazing only 50 metres away. The lioness and her family had not eaten for a week. She had not made a kill in her last four chases. If she failed to get a meal for her cubs now, they would certainly die from starvation.

The lioness moved silently on her padded paws. She had been following the gnu for two hours. Only now was she close enough to pounce. She was not as fast as the gnu and she did not have as much stamina. So the success of her attack would depend on surprise.

Suddenly the lioness charged, sprinting across the ground at about 35 kilometres an hour. She quickly caught up with the terrified gnu and sent it crashing to the ground. The lioness sank her strong, dagger-like teeth into the gnu's throat, and then used her front legs to strangle the gnu [Fig. 2]. After about five minutes, the gnu was dead.

The lioness dragged the body to her family. She began eating greedily, keeping the hungry cubs away. The male lion soon arrived. He was the

Fig. 2 A lioness with her latest catch. Each lioness kills about 20 herbivores per year. Statistically, a gnu is as much at risk of being eaten by a lion as you are of being knocked down and killed by a car

boss and pushed the lioness away. He ate the 'lion's share' of the kill. This was about 234 kilograms of meat—about one-fifth of his own weight. The lioness then took her share.

Finally, it was the turn of the cubs. The whole meal took about 50 minutes to finish. The satisfied family rested in full view of the herd of gnus which had provided them with their latest meal. Very soon, a group of hyenas tackled the remainder of the carcass. And vultures flew overhead waiting to pounce. By the end of the day, all that was left of the victim were a few bones and four hooves.

Bed bug

These animals feed on blood. They have special mouthparts to prick the skin. They also have a special chemical in their saliva to stop blood clotting as they suck blood through the skin. A bed bug is an example of a **parasite**—it feeds on other living things which are called **hosts**. You can read more about parasites in *6 Living together*.

Lioness

Lions must eat meat to survive and are called **carnivores**. Lionesses rely on the strength of their teeth for hunting. The digestive system of carnivores is designed for digesting meat and will not deal with plants.

Fig. 3 The gnu

1 Food is swallowed into the **rumen**.
2 Later it is regurgitated, chewed and passed to the **reticulum**.
3 This reswallowed food is passed to the **omasum** where water is reabsorbed.
4 Digestion is completed in the **abomasum** and intestines.

Gnu

The gnu feeds on plants and is called a **herbivore**. Its teeth are suited to tearing the kind of plants which grow where it lives. It is also a **ruminant**. Ruminants are animals with stomachs containing four separate chambers [Fig. 3]. In the first chamber, which is called the rumen, the hurriedly eaten food is stored. When the rumen is filled, the animal can move away quickly if danger threatens. In the rumen, the food is moistened with fluids containing millions of bacteria. The bacteria break down cellulose from the plants into other substances. Later, the food is returned to the mouth and chewed for a long time before being passed to the other chambers for digestion to be completed.

QUESTIONS
1 Why are the teeth of the gnu and the lioness so different?
2 The eyes of the gnu are on the sides of its head whereas the eyes of the lioness are much closer together at the front of the head. In each case explain how these arrangements help the survival of the animal.
3 How do you think that a bed bug can sense the presence of a human being such as John?
4 Why is it that a bed bug may have a long time to wait in between meals?
5 A bed bug relies indirectly on plants for its food. Can you explain why?

6 Living together

There are many examples of pairs of unrelated animals and plants which live close to each other in a partnership. Sometimes the partnership is very close and permanent and each partner benefits from the presence of the other. This is called **symbiosis**. Another kind of partnership is called **parasitism**. In this case, one partner, called the **parasite**, lives at the expense of the other partner, called the **host**.

In this chapter you will read about some examples of symbiosis and parasitism.

A touching moment

Mrs Thomson was seething! The school nurse had just visited: Susan had head lice! She had washed Susan's hair only yesterday. Susan must have been infected by dirty children at school. Then Mrs Thomson remembered the nurse saying that head lice were not really dirty. They are just a nuisance. She began to read the leaflet which the nurse had given to her.

She read that although head lice are more common in children, adults can also carry the louse. She scratched her head at the thought.

Mrs Thomson took the lid off the bottle the nurse had given her. The lotion inside was very smelly, but the nurse had said that it really did work. Ordinary shampoos just keep the lice clean, she had emphasised, and an insecticide was needed to kill the lice and destroy their eggs. The lotion had to be left on the hair for twelve hours before using a normal shampoo.

Mrs Thomson scratched her head again and smiled! Perhaps she would not complain to the school and, yes, she would certainly treat the whole family. They had probably all become infested as they had put their heads together over a jigsaw puzzle last week. She had not realised before that lice could walk from one head to another so easily. She would also make certain that they combed their hair regularly and thoroughly too. She had remembered reading that funny notice about lice being injured by combing and the slogan 'If you break lice legs, they can't lay eggs'.

WHY PUT UP WITH UNWANTED GUESTS?

Treatment is pleasant and simple - ask your chemist or clinic for advice

The head louse is a parasite of humans. The louse is a greyish insect which lives on the scalp [Fig. 1]. Here the hair provides the ideal place to lay eggs. The temperature is just right and food is plentiful. All the louse has to do to feed is to bite the scalp and suck up blood!

The female louse lays about six eggs during the night, sticking each one to a separate hair with a kind of glue. A young louse hatches out after a week leaving behind an egg case still glued to the hair. Lice eggs are sometimes confused with dandruff. But dandruff is flaky whereas lice eggs, or 'nits' as they are often called, have an oval shape.

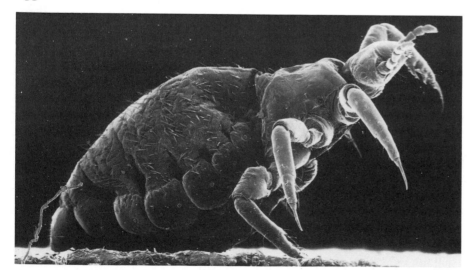

Fig. 1 A head louse

Apples, parasites and supermarkets

Tim Bevelay was doing the family shopping in the new supermarket. High on the list was fresh fruit. His father reminded him again about choosing fruit as he left home.

'Don't go picking up the first apples you see. Have a good look and make sure none of them have any marks!' he had said.

By the fruit counter Tim could see lots of shoppers doing just that.

'I wonder what happens to fruit with marks on the skin', he thought, 'and I wonder if marks make the fruit poisonous or something!'

We all like to see 'perfect' apples and pears, and shops try to supply perfect fruit for us. So growers take care that their fruit is well protected from diseases and parasites. One common way of protecting fruit is to spray the trees regularly to keep away parasites. One of the parasites affecting apples is **apple scab**.

Apple scab is a disease carried by a fungus. Young leaves become covered in black spots, and blisters appear on the bark of young shoots. Eventually, the apples are affected and black spots appear on their skins. The skins then crack, making the apples unfit for storage.

There are far more scabs on the red sides of apples facing outwards from the tree than on the inward-facing green sides. When it rains, water runs off the green parts quickly, but tends to linger on the red side. This is because there is more water-repellent wax on the green skin than the red skin. Spores causing apple scab are spread by rain splashes, and tend to gather on the red side. So fungal growth is more common here than on the green side.

You can see in Fig. 2 how the apple scab fungus affects a tree during the year. Many marks on fruit are not harmful, but 'perfect' fruit sells at the highest prices. It is important to wash fruit well before eating to remove as much as possible of the chemicals which have been sprayed onto the fruit by the growers.

On the rocks

It was lunchtime on a cold autumn day on the west coast of Scotland. Alan and his friend Mark were making their way to the top of a rock face about 800 metres above sea level.

Mark said, 'It's not surprising that little grows up here. Look how far we've climbed above those old oak trees. Even the grass is thin here.'

'There will soon be no grass either,' said Alan. 'Look at the big rock face up there. Nothing will grow on that.'

But as they reached the rock face, they noticed that it was covered with grey-green and orange patches [Fig. 3].

'What is this stuff on the rocks?' asked Alan. 'Is it moss? How on earth does it manage to survive here in this wind and cold?'

'It's not moss, it's a lichen,' said Mark. A lichen consists of lots of minute plants growing inside a fungus. The plants make food for themselves and the fungus, while the fungus protects the plants.'

'It works well,' said Alan, 'otherwise it would never grow *here*. Talking about food and protection, I'm hungry. You get the food ready and I'll put up the tent.'

The plant part of a lichen is a single-celled **alga**. Like all plants, algae make carbohydrates by photosynthesis. The fungus part, in turn, protects the algal cells from strong sunlight and extremes of temperature and gives them moisture. The plant and fungus help each other to survive. They are partners in **symbiosis**. The word symbiosis comes from the Greek word meaning 'living together'. The two boys are also helping each other in the same kind of way.

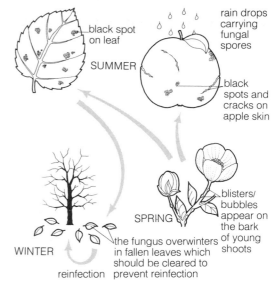

Fig. 2 Life cycle of the fungus causing apple scab

Fig. 3 Lichens are the first arrivals on bare rock

QUESTIONS

1 Explain the difference between symbiosis and parasitism.

2 List two further examples of parasitism and two of symbiosis.

3 We pay more for our fresh fruit because sprays are used to keep the fruit as 'perfect' as possible. Do you agree that sprays should be used for this reason? Explain your answer.

4 Read the last part of 'On the rocks' again. Explain the link between symbiosis in lichens and what the boys are doing.

5 A survey taken in Great Britain indicated that lichens were common in the southwest of England and in northern Scotland. They were scarce in the more heavily populated parts of Britain. What sort of conditions do you think lichens grow best in?

15

7 Storing food

Read this list: smoked bacon, pickled onions, dried peas, baked beans, canned peaches, salted herrings, frozen chips, pasteurised milk, boiled eggs, potato crisps, roasted peanuts.

All of these foods have been **processed** in some way to **preserve** them. If you think about all the different foods you eat, very few are eaten 'fresh'. This chapter is about some of the methods of processing food.

Why is food processed?

Most of us live in large towns or cities far away from where our food is grown or reared. Most of what we eat has to be transported from different parts of the country to our shops before we can buy it [Fig. 1]. A lot of food has to be imported from overseas. Importing takes time. For example, New Zealand lamb takes several weeks to reach Britain by ship. Many of the vegetables we eat are harvested in their season. But we like to eat them all the year round.

People are eating more 'convenience' food like ready-cooked meats and chips. They only need heating before being served. When we buy food and take it home, we do not eat it all at once but store it until required.

In all cases, food is being stored before being eaten. Unless food is carefully processed and preserved, it will spoil before it reaches you. Spoiled food is unpleasant and may be unsafe to eat.

Why does food spoil?

Fruit and vegetables ripen because **enzymes** are at work inside them. The enzymes may continue to work after the food has been picked. You may have put green tomatoes on a windowsill so that they will turn red and ripen in the sun. The flavour of tomatoes is then improved. But some foods, for example strawberries and raspberries, deteriorate quickly after picking. They need to be processed quickly to kill the enzymes.

Once plant and animal material is killed, it can no longer prevent attack by microorganisms. Some microorganisms spoil food by breaking it down and making nasty flavours and smells. They can also cause illness if they multiply in food which is later eaten.

So ways are needed to stop microorganisms from attacking food. Modern methods of food processing retain the quality and appearance of food for a long period of time. However, you should realise that preserving food has been done for many years. Wheat has been processed into flour for centuries, hops have been added to beer to preserve it, and pork has been cured to provide bacon.

Dehydration

Microorganisms and enzymes are inactivated by removing almost all the water from food. This process, called **dehydration**, is used to produce 'dried' foods. Peas are dried by this process. They are first '**blanched**' by plunging them into boiling water to stop enzymes working. They are then treated with dilute sulphuric acid to extend storage life. The air temperature is gradually raised as the peas are dried. At the end of the process the peas have a 5% content of water.

Fig. 1 Supermarket shelves are full of preserved food

Quick freezing

The activity of microorganisms is reduced by refrigeration and totally stopped at temperatures between -5 and $-20°C$. Food used to be frozen slowly, but this was found to be unsatisfactory [Fig. 2(a)] because large ice crystals formed which ruptured the cells. When the food was thawed, water would drain away, carrying valuable salts and minerals with it. In the 1920's, Clarence Birdseye (recognise the brand name?) noticed that eskimos stored frozen fish in the open air for several months and then thawed and ate it as though it was fresh. From his observations he introduced 'quick freezing'. When this occurs the ice crystals which form are very small and do not damage the cells of frozen food [Fig. 2(b)].

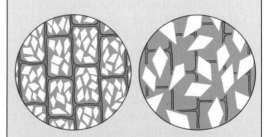

Fig. 2 The advantage of quick freezing

(a) Large crystals are formed when the food is frozen slowly and the cell walls are ruptured

(b) Small ice crystals are formed in quick-frozen food

How do baked beans get into the tin?

Look at Figs. 3–5 showing how baked beans are produced.

The process begins with dried beans. As with peas, drying helps to stop the beans from being spoiled during storage. Look at the box in Fig. 5 about **blanching**. Beans are blanched in water at 95°C to destroy enzymes. (Fresh vegetables are blanched before being stored in house freezers for the same reason.)

Now look at the last box but one. The tins of beans are heated by steam to 115°C to sterilise the contents. All food in cans and bottles is sterilised by heating. Canned fruit is sterilised at the lower temperature of 100°C because acid in the fruit helps to limit the growth of microorganisms. But meat and fish must be sterilised at 121°C. Some foods preserved by canning and bottling have been edible after 100 years, so the process works well! But take care not to buy damaged cans. It is possible that the contents may have reacted with the metal of the can where it has been damaged. This may have let microorganisms from the air enter the can.

Fig. 3 Navy bean pods, from which baked beans are made

Fig. 4 Part of the production line in a baked bean factory

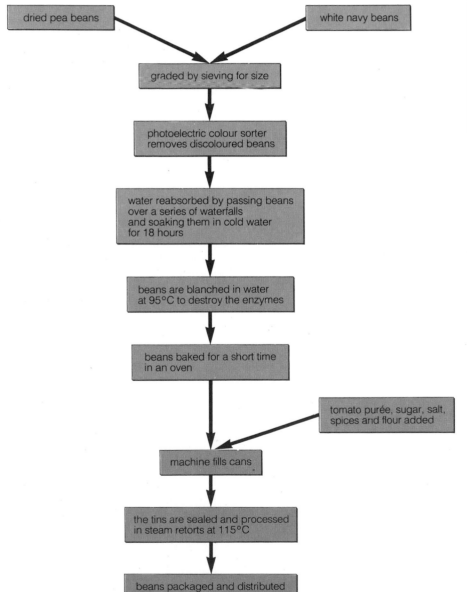

Fig. 5 How baked beans are processed

8 Fungi and bacteria–friends or enemies?

Fungi and bacteria survive in all parts of the world from the coldest regions to the hottest. They can be found in the air, soil or water. While some fungi and bacteria are harmful and can kill us, there are many more that are helpful to us.

Harmful fungi

Diseases caused by fungi are not common in humans. The best known is **ringworm**. This fungus can spread over the skin and cause irritation and inflammation. When ringworm appears between the toes it is known as **athlete's foot**. You can see the effect in Fig. 1. Although the disease is not very dangerous, it can split the skin and allow harmful microorganisms to enter the body.

Harmful bacteria

Harmful bacteria can invade the body through the air you breathe, in your food and drink or through wounds in your skin. Once inside your body, the bacteria can take the nutrients they need from your tissues.

Bacteria may cause disease by destroying cells so that the body organs are weakened and unable to work properly. But the main damage is caused by the chemical substances which bacteria release during their growth and development. These chemicals are poisonous and are called **toxins**. Fig. 2 shows some harmful bacteria and the diseases which they cause.

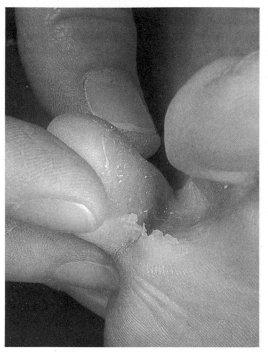

Fig. 1 Athlete's foot

Fig. 2 Some disease-causing bacteria

Disease	Tetanus	Typhoid	Syphilis	Cholera	Pneumonia	Boils
Type of bacterium	*Bacillus*	*Bacillus*	*Spirillum*	*Vibrio*	*Diplococcus*	*Staphylococcus*
Method of entry into body	bacteria enter wounds	eating food or fluid containing bacteria	sexual contact	waterborne	airborne	airborne/ direct contact
Effects	muscle spasms and paralysis, lockjaw	diarrhoea and fever	sores in genital region; in later stage the nervous system affected. Can be passed to baby by an infected mother	diarrhoea; severe water loss can cause death	coughing; chest pains; fluid in lungs	inflammation and pus formation in local regions

Helpful fungi and bacteria

Fig. 3 gives some of the uses of helpful fungi and bacteria.

Recycling by fungi and bacteria

The activity of fungi, bacteria and small animals decomposes the leaves which fall from trees each autumn. Dead plants still contain large quantities of energy and raw materials which would be lost forever if they were not broken down. Bacteria and fungi are the only organisms which can decompose dead substances. Simple compounds which bacteria and fungi release from dead material are absorbed by plants through their roots. So bacteria and fungi help to recycle raw materials.

If there were no fungi and bacteria, the whole living world would be piled high with dead plants and animals and their waste products.

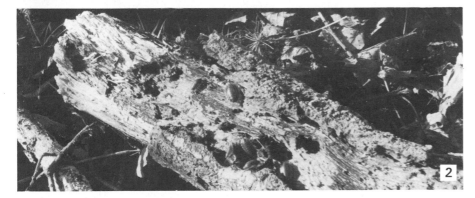

The story of a fallen branch

1   When a branch falls to the ground [Fig. 4], the leaves are quickly broken up and eaten by scavengers such as snails, millipedes, woodlice and earthworms. Earthworms digest most of the cellulose in the leaves but the rest of the leaf matter passes through as faeces. The faeces are then decomposed by bacteria. If the leaves are moist, fungi and bacteria begin to feed on them directly. The fungi and bacteria secrete digestive enzymes onto the leaves. The enzymes break down the cellulose and lignin into simple substances, such as sugars, which are absorbed by the bacteria and fungi. Fungi and bacteria which feed on dead organic matter are called **saprophytes**.
2   Beetles loosen the bark and bore into the sapwood. Woodlice and millipedes can then enter the branch and break the wood into small pieces. Bacteria and fungi decompose the wood and hasten its decay.

Fungi penetrate deeper and deeper into the wood for several years. Meanwhile, craneflies, stag beetles and click beetles lay eggs in the rotting wood. The larvae eat the rotting wood and burrow into it.

Fig. 3 Uses of fungi and bacteria

Uses of bacteria

1 In the intestines of herbivores to break down the cellulose in plant food.
2 In the soil to change nitrogen in the atmosphere into nitrates which plants need to grow.
3 In the making of cheese and yoghurt.
4 In sewage works to break down harmful chemicals into less harmful substances.

Uses of fungi

1 Yeast is used to make bread dough rise.
2 In brewing to make alcohol.
3 In cheese to make it mature more quickly and improve the flavour.
4 To make penicillin, an antibiotic.

Fig. 4 The decay of a fallen branch

QUESTIONS
1 How does the body defend itself against infection by bacteria?
2 Under ideal conditions a bacterium will divide every twenty minutes or so. This rarely happens. Why not?
3 A piece of moist bread and a piece of dry bread were placed in sealed jars and left for fourteen days. After this time it was noticed that the moist bread was mouldy but the dry bread was not. Explain these observations.
4 A similar experiment to the one above was carried out, but the jars were placed in a refrigerator. After fourteen days, what results would you expect and why?
5 All the leaves that fall from trees in the autumn seem to disappear. Explain what really happens to them.

9 Why have blood?

The body has many different organs. Each organ has a special job to do. For example, the lungs take oxygen from the air and allow carbon dioxide to escape from the body. But all the organs of the body have one thing in common: organs are made from cells and every cell needs energy from food to do work. So food has to reach every cell. Oxygen is also needed by every cell to allow energy to be released from the food.

It is the blood which carries food and oxygen round the body. The blood also carries many other substances vital to the body. In this chapter you will read about the blood system.

What is blood?

Blood looks like a red liquid but it is made of these main parts:

Plasma   This is a pale yellow liquid. Plasma carries food and special chemicals round the body. It also carries two kinds of cells.

Red cells   The red colour of blood comes from the **red cells** [Fig. 1]. There are about 5 million red cells per cubic millimetre of blood. Red cells carry oxygen around the body using a substance called **haemoglobin**.

White cells   The white cells are larger than red cells and protect the body from infection [Fig. 2]. There are fewer white cells than red cells.

The plasma also contains **platelets** which help blood to clot if it escapes from the body. Clotting reduces the loss of blood if you cut yourself. It also helps to stop microorganisms from entering the body.

Many special chemicals are carried in the plasma including **hormones**. Hormones regulate some of the chemical changes in the body.

How does blood move around the body?

Blood flows around the body in **arteries** and **veins**. These are narrow tubes which connect all the different parts of the body in a huge network. Arteries carry blood away from the heart. They divide into smaller and smaller tubes until they reach the **capillaries**. You have more than 96 500 km of capillaries in your body! And none of your body cells are more than 0·13 millimetres from a capillary. The blood passes slowly through the capillaries and allows substances to move to and from the cells and blood. Blood returns to the heart through the **veins**.

Understanding blood flow

In the sixteenth century, people believed that blood just 'ebbed and flowed' backwards and forwards in the body. But a very famous doctor called William Harvey used scientific experiments to show how blood really did flow around the body.

William Harvey was doctor to King Charles I and served him during the war between the King and Parliament. In 1628, William Harvey

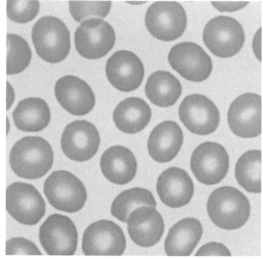

Fig. 1 Red blood cells

Fig. 2 White cell engulfing a bacterium

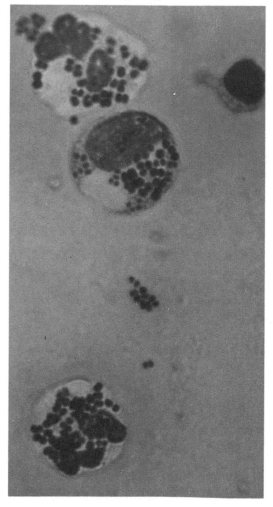

wrote a book on the circulation of blood which made him world famous. Look at the diagram [Fig. 3] showing one of his experiments.

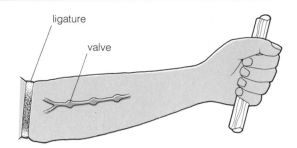

ligature

valve

1 He tied a tight bandage called a **ligature** above the elbow of a patient. He noticed small swellings in the veins. These swellings were places where there were **valves** in the veins below the ligature. (He had examined such valves before and knew that they only allowed blood to flow in one direction.)

2 He placed one finger at A and pushed blood with another finger towards the shoulder and past a valve at B.

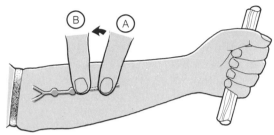

Finger Ⓑ pushes blood towards the shoulder from Ⓐ to Ⓑ

3 He released his finger from B but kept his other finger at A. Blood did *not* flow back again to A. But when he removed his finger from A, blood flowed into the empty vein and up to B.

Harvey concluded that the normal direction of blood flow in veins of the arm is towards the shoulder. He carried out many experiments and dissected many animal and human bodies to study their anatomy. His description of blood circulation is still believed to be correct.

In his work, Harvey always used these steps: careful observation, careful thought, a good experiment, and thorough analysis of its results. His methods have been followed by scientists ever since.

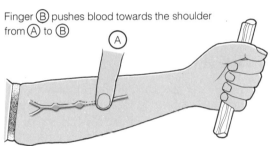

Release finger Ⓑ. Blood does not flow back towards Ⓐ
When finger Ⓐ is removed blood flows into empty vein from Ⓐ to Ⓑ

Fig. 3 Harvey's experiment

The blood system

The blood system is a little like the central heating system in a house. Blood is like the water flowing round. The arteries and veins in which blood flows are like the pipes. And the heart which pumps the blood is like the water pump. Look at the pipes and boxes in Fig. 4. Follow the arrows as blood leaves the heart by the left ventricle (LV) in the arteries to the body tissues. After oxygen has been given up, blood flows in the veins until it reaches the right auricle (RA) of the heart. It is then pumped to the lungs where it collects oxygen and returns to the left auricle (LA) of the heart. It then leaves to flow around the body again.

Fig. 4 The circulation of blood around the body

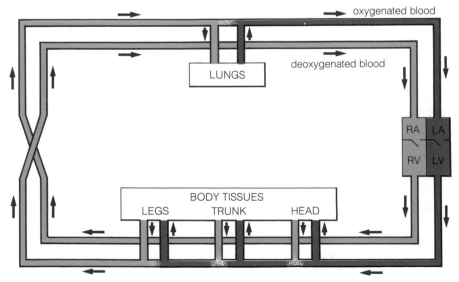

oxygenated blood

deoxygenated blood

LUNGS

RA | LA
RV | LV

BODY TISSUES
LEGS   TRUNK   HEAD

QUESTIONS

1 Make a list of the names of three kinds of 'tubes' in the body through which blood flows.
   (a) Which tubes carry blood towards the heart?
   (b) Which tubes have the smallest diameter?

2 Explain in your own words what Harvey concluded about blood flow from his experiment.

3 How do the pipes in a central heating system differ from the 'tubes' in the blood system?

4 Compare the operation of a pump in a central heating system with the pumping of the heart.

5 Why do you think it would be inefficient if we had water circulating through our tubes instead of blood?

10 The story of a recovery

John was twelve when it all happened. Just before starting the new term at school, he began to suffer from diarrhoea. The family doctor was soon contacted but was not alarmed. A few days later, blood began to appear in the faeces. The doctor sent John to a big city hospital to seek advice from a surgeon who had helped many patients with problems in their digestive systems [Fig. 1].

John was admitted to hospital and several tests were carried out. His blood was analysed to check the concentration of red blood cells and his body temperature was taken. His abdomen was then pressed in to check for any pain. Finally, a sample of his faeces was analysed for signs of disease in his digestive system.

The surgeon checked the results and soon explained that John was suffering from **colitis**, which is a very rare disease in young people. He drew a diagram to help him explain the effect of the disease on the body.

The digestive system

Look at the diagram of the digestive system [Fig. 2]. It shows the **stomach** leading to the **small intestine**, the connection to the **colon** with the appendix at the junction, the colon itself and, finally, the **rectum** and anus. The surgeon explained the function of each part.

When food is swallowed, it soon reaches the stomach where it is churned by powerful muscles in the stomach wall. A **sphincter muscle**, which is a kind of valve, opens occasionally and allows food to be squirted into the small intestine.

As food moves along the small intestine, digestive juices make the food soluble so that it can be absorbed by blood flowing through the walls. Food spends about 8 hours in passing through the small intestine which is about 5 metres long.

By the time food reaches the colon, almost all the useful parts have been digested and so removed. The main purpose of the colon is to absorb water from the waste substances. After passing through the colon, which is about 1·5 metres long, the waste is stored in the rectum before being released as faeces through the anus. Faeces consist mainly of bacteria, which live in the colon, some undigested food, dead cells from the walls of the small intestine and colon, and waste from dead blood cells.

Colitis

John had a disease of the colon called **colitis** which attacks the inner wall of the colon and can cause holes through the wall. He was kept in hospital and drank liquid food which could be digested easily. The idea was to reduce the waste passing through the colon. He was given a large dose of steroid drugs to reduce the effects of the colitis. His condition improved and he left hospital after three weeks.

The drugs made his cheeks swell and his friends called him 'secret squirrel', although he felt very well. But as the dose of drugs was decreased, his colon became worse. He returned to hospital for an operation called an **ileostomy**. His abdomen was opened and a cut was made in his colon near the junction with the small intestine. The loose

Fig. 1 John was admitted to hospital for tests

end of the small intestine was then brought outside his body through his abdomen. This allowed all the waste material to drain outside his body and gave his colon a complete rest.

The surgeon hoped that he could re-connect the colon when it had fully recovered. But after 10 months, no real improvement had occurred. The only solution left was to remove the whole of the colon and rectum. In a long and difficult operation, this was done. John's appendix was also removed. Finally, the small intestine was joined directly to the anus.

Fig. 2 The digestive system

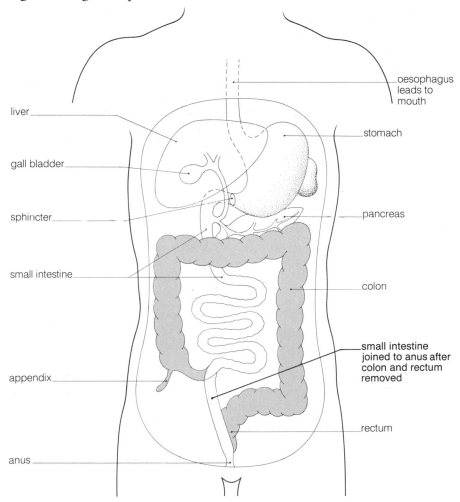

liver
gall bladder
sphincter
small intestine
appendix
anus

oesophagus leads to mouth
stomach
pancreas
colon
small intestine joined to anus after colon and rectum removed
rectum

 This part of digestive system removed in an operation

Fig. 3 John is now a healthy teenager

Adjusting to change

With no colon or rectum, John had two main problems: water was not being reabsorbed by a colon and there was no rectum in which to store waste matter. For the first few days, liquid waste left the anus every hour both day and night. But with the help of harmless drugs, his body began to adjust. After three months, it was every four hours and after one year, every six hours. His control of waste was improving. After two years he did not need to take any drugs.

He is now a healthy and growing teenager [Fig. 3].

QUESTIONS
1 Describe in your own words how unwanted materials in the food we eat pass from the mouth to the anus.
2 What is the main function of the colon? How does the removal of the colon affect the body?
3 Why are faeces still formed even when all the food eaten is digested?
4 Why do you think that John's appendix was removed during the operation?
5 Why do you think that it took so long for John's body to readjust after his operation? Do you think that John should go to the doctor for regular check ups?

11 When things go wrong

When we feel ill we go to a doctor. The doctor first asks you to describe **symptoms**, such as dizziness and aches, and looks for **signs**, such as spots and high temperature. The doctor works out what may be the problem. He or she tries to work out a **diagnosis** (or theory) of the problem from the symptoms and signs. The doctor then tries out a **treatment** on you. If the treatment works, you will be cured. If the treatment does not work, the doctor examines you carefully again and tries out a new treatment.

You can now read two stories of people who were ill and were cured.

Sandra Johnson

Sandra Johnson was forty-eight and worked as a shop manager. She was normally quite fit and active but had become troubled with bronchitis. Sandra had been smoking about 20 cigarettes a day for 30 years. She had tried to stop smoking several times but had not succeeded.

On 10 March, Sandra caught a bad head cold. On 12 March, she began to cough and the coughing caused a slight pain down the middle of the front of her chest. By 14 March, the cough had become worse. She had bought a cough medicine from the chemist but it had not helped. She decided to visit her doctor.

Dr Brook carefully noted her **symptoms** and asked Sandra if she had recently met anybody with colds or diseases. He looked at her throat for **signs** of redness which would indicate infection, and listened to her chest with his stethoscope [Fig. 1]. The sounds through a stethoscope can show up problems in the working of the heart and lungs. In Sandra's case, there were abnormal sounds as air entered and left the lower left lung. Dr Brook **diagnosed** bronchitis caused by a virus which was linked with the head cold. Normally, this would not be serious, but Sandra was a heavy smoker. He was concerned that the lung damage caused by the bronchitis might lead to further damage by bacteria.

This is the treatment prescribed by Dr Brook:

1 An antibiotic for five days to destroy or prevent the growth of bacteria.
2 A linctus to soothe the cough.
3 An analgesic to relieve aches and pains.

By 18 March, Sandra's symptoms had got worse and Dr Brook was called to visit her. He discovered that the signs of bronchitis had become worse. He also found that her temperature had reached 39·5°C. He diagnosed **bronchopneumonia** and sent her to hospital.

At hospital, the House Doctor examined Sandra and asked for a chest X-ray, a blood count and a bacterial culture of sputum to be carried out. Without waiting for the results, she prescribed two different antibiotics which would kill almost all bacteria which are the cause of bronchopneumonia.

By 20 March, Sandra felt much better. The cough had loosened, the fever had passed and the aches and pains had gone. The X-ray had shown a thickening of parts of the lower left lung that is found in bronchopneumonia [Fig. 2]. The blood cell count had shown an increase in the number of white cells. (This increase usually occurs when bacteria

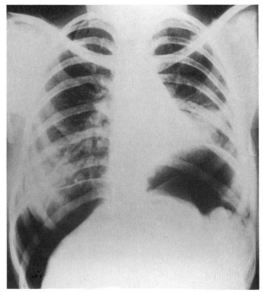

Fig. 1 The doctor used a stethoscope to listen to Sandra's chest

Fig. 2 Bronchopneumonia in a lung (x-ray photo)

cause infection.) The sputum culture did not produce any bacteria linked with the infection.

Sandra continued to improve and left hospital on 21 March. She was advised to continue her treatment for four days and to give up smoking. One week later she had fully recovered and had stopped smoking. She was fine except for problems caused by giving up smoking.

Alan Robinson

Alan Robinson was fifty-five and was a bank manager. He had always been fit and played amateur football until he was forty-two. But he had noticed that he became quite breathless after mowing the lawn and that his ankles were swelling in the evening. He decided to visit his doctor.

Dr Slade asked Alan to describe his **symptoms**. She made a careful note of the symptoms and then checked Alan's medical records. About 15 years earlier the doctor had heard a slightly strange sound through her stethoscope when examining Alan. She had **diagnosed** this as a heart murmur but took no action at the time. About 30 years ago Alan had developed rheumatic fever after a bout of tonsillitis.

Dr Slade then carried out these tests on Alan:

1 She found Alan's heart rate normal at 70 beats per minute, and the force of his pulse was average.
2 His blood pressure (150/85) was slightly higher than 15 years before but this was to be expected for his age.
3 She examined Alan's skin but there was no swelling even though his ankles became swollen at night.
4 When she listened to Alan's heart, she heard abnormal sounds from the closing of the mitral valve. The valve is between the right auricle and right ventricle. It sounded as if the valve had narrowed. This problem is called **mitral stenosis**.
5 Dr Slade listened with her stethoscope to sounds from Alan's lungs. It sounded as if fluid was collecting at the bottom of his right lung. This problem is often linked with mitral stenosis.

Dr Slade advised Alan to rest at home until he could see a heart specialist at the local hospital. She was concerned because the flow of blood through the heart is reduced with mitral stenosis.

Mr Shah at the hospital gave Alan the same tests as had Dr Slade. But he also asked for a chest X-ray and an electrocardiogram (ECG) [Fig. 3]. Mr Shah did not expect these tests to show anything abnormal. But he wanted to check if anything else was wrong with Alan's heart. Mr Shah confirmed Dr Slade's diagnosis of mitral stenosis. Damage had been caused to Alan's mitral valve when he had rheumatic fever 30 years before.

Four days later, Alan was given a general anaesthetic and linked to a heart–lung machine. Mr Shah could then work on Alan's heart without the heart having to pump blood around the body. Mr Shah removed the damaged mitral valve and replaced it with a plastic valve [Fig. 4].

In 24 hours Alan was walking around. In six weeks he returned to work at the bank.

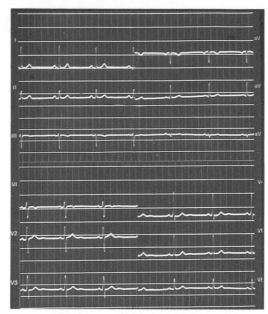
Fig. 3 Electrocardiogram of a normal heart

Fig. 4 An artificial heart valve

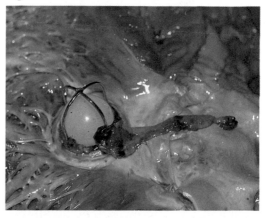

QUESTIONS

1 For each of the stories in this chapter, make up a table with six column headings:
  1 Symptoms
  2 Tests
  3 Diagnosis
  4 Treatment
  5 Result
  6 Conclusions
  and fill it in. Use the table to compare the success of Dr Brook and Dr Slade in diagnosing the problem.
2 Why did the House Doctor at the hospital take Sandra's blood count?
3 What other major illnesses might smoking make worse?
4 What problems are caused for people who give up smoking?

12 How do babies survive?

The birth of a healthy, wanted baby is a very happy event. Very few babies born in Britain die before their first birthday. This is mainly due to the care women receive during pregnancy and the kinds of food, love and attention babies receive after birth. Read this story about a baby born in Britain. You can then think more about the problems faced by babies in other parts of the world.

A happy event

Lucy's doctor had confirmed her hopes; she was going to have a baby! The doctor had tested a urine sample to confirm her pregnancy. He had also sent a blood sample to the laboratory to find the blood group to which she belonged. The laboratory would also check if she was anaemic and if she had syphilis.

The doctor gave Lucy general advice about keeping in good health during her pregnancy. She was advised not to smoke because smoking increases the risk of miscarriage and of the baby being smaller at birth than it should be. The doctor also advised her to avoid drinking too much alcohol and not to take any drugs unless prescribed by him.

Lucy decided to take care with her diet and not to 'eat for two'. Instead she planned a balanced diet with sufficient protein and no excess fat or carbohydrates. She knew that she should not gain more than 12 kg while she was pregnant. More than this might cause high blood pressure. Lucy decided to drink a daily pint of milk and to eat plenty of fresh fruit and vegetables. These foods would provide the calcium and vitamins that she and her baby would need.

Peter, Lucy's husband, wanted her to take things very easily, but this was not necessary. Exercise, particularly swimming, is good during pregnancy as long as it is not too strenuous and does not involve lifting heavy weights. Sleep is very important and Lucy was advised to sleep eight and a half hours each night. She decided to make a dental appointment which was free now she was pregnant. Teeth decay more quickly during pregnancy and gum disease is more likely to occur.

Lucy enjoyed meeting other expectant mothers at the antenatal clinic a month later. The midwife again examined Lucy and checked her blood pressure and urine. Lucy was asked to attend the clinic every month. She could then be checked regularly to see that her pregnancy was normal. She would also be taught about the birth and how to look after her baby.

Nine months later

Lucy and Peter's tiny baby was a big responsibility. He depended totally on them for food, warmth and love. They had not realised how much work would be needed in looking after all his needs but found this experience rewarding. Lucy had decided to breast feed her baby. The first milk produced by the breast is called **colostrum**. This milk contains all the food a newborn baby needs. It has five times more protein than normal breast milk, and less fat. After two or three days, proper breast milk is produced.

At first, babies may want to feed every twenty minutes! They know when they are hungry just like everyone else. Lucy wondered if she

Fig. 1 The advantages and disadvantages of breast and bottle feeding

Breast milk	Artificial milk
Carbohydrate, protein and fat content	
Ideal, so most is absorbed	Less well absorbed
Mineral content	
Ideal	Ideal, if correct amount, diluted accurately, is given
Vitamin content	
Lacking vitamin A. Vitamin drops available from clinic	Ideal as vitamins are added
Concentration	
Strength is regulated naturally	Strength is constant
Nourishment	
Ideal. However, if mother produces too little, the baby will fail to gain weight	It is easier to overfeed the baby and make it overweight
Protection against infections	
Natural antibodies in the milk provide protection, particularly against chest and intestinal infections	Provides no protection
Protection against other illnesses	
Possibly provides protection against eczema and asthma	Provides no protection. Can cause diarrhoea, skin rashes or chest illnesses
Contamination of milk	
Not possible	Bottles must be cleaned and sterilised, otherwise bacteria may cause diarrhoea
Convenience	
No equipment needed. Only mother can feed the baby	Considerable equipment needed. Father or others can feed the baby
Expense	
None	Considerable
Supply	
May diminish if mother is tired or ill	Always available

would have enough milk to satisfy her baby. But she soon learned that breasts supply as much as the baby takes. The more milk the baby took the more milk was produced. She sometimes wished that she or Peter could feed the baby with a bottle. But she knew how much better breast milk is for a baby than artificial milk. You can compare the two kinds of milk in the table [Fig. 1].

Just like adults, babies vary in the amount of sleep they need. New-born babies spend most of the time asleep. The amount of sleep decreases as they get older. When Lucy's baby was awake, he needed someone to play with him. Lucy enjoyed this and knew that she was helping him to learn and develop properly.

Lucy took her baby to the child health clinic every two weeks at first. The health visitor weighed him and asked Lucy to collect vitamin drops. Breastfed babies often need extra vitamins.

When Lucy's baby was three months old, he had his first injection to protect him against several diseases. Look at the full immunisation plan [Fig. 2]. Babies and children have injections in the plan until they reach sixteen years of age.

Age	Immunisation given
3–6 months	1 Diphtheria, whooping cough, tetanus, polio
4–6 weeks later	2 Diphtheria, whooping cough, tetanus, polio
4–6 weeks later	3 Diphtheria, whooping cough, tetanus, polio
1–2 years	Measles
4–5 years	Diphtheria, tetanus, polio
10–13 years	BCG vaccination against TB if skin test negative
11–14 years	Rubella (German measles) – girls only
15 years	Tetanus and polio

Fig. 2 The immunisation programme

Fig. 3 Infant mortality in the world today

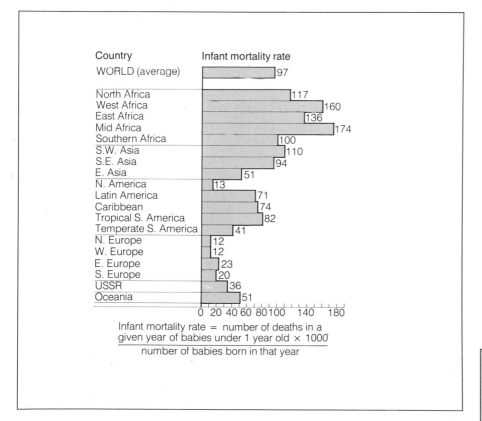

Infant mortality rate = number of deaths in a given year of babies under 1 year old × 1000 / number of babies born in that year

Infant mortality

You have read in the story about the care given to expectant mothers and babies. In spite of all this care, about 12 babies in every thousand die in Britain before they reach their first birthday. But in 1870, as many as 225 babies in every thousand died. The table shows the infant mortality rate for many parts of the world [Fig. 3]. You can see that the rate in parts of Africa is almost as high now as it was in Britain a hundred years ago. Many of the early deaths in Africa are due to malnutrition.

You can read more about malnutrition in *28 Feeding the World*, and about plans for saving children in *30 Saving the world's children*.

QUESTIONS

1 Why did Lucy's doctor test a urine sample?
2 Why was Lucy advised to stop smoking?
3 Describe Lucy's diet. Why did she eat fruit and fresh vegetables?
4 Describe in your own words, six advantages of breast feeding.
5 Use the table to make a list of all the injections you should have received. Put a cross by any which you have not received. Then make a list of all the diseases which you have had. Compare your list with other members of your class.

13 Muscle power

When you run, walk or move your body in any other way, you are using your muscles. You have about 600 muscles in your body and all are controlled by your brain. Even in simple movements, many muscles have to work together. In all movements, your brain allows for the force of gravity acting on all parts of your body. Your body has to be 'in balance' with the force of gravity or else you would fall over! Athletes, such as weightlifters and bodybuilders train and develop their bodies for special movements and are able to control their muscles well [Fig. 1].

The skill of a weightlifter

You may have enjoyed watching weightlifters lifting huge weights and noticed their muscular bodies [Fig. 2]. A weightlifter needs great strength to lift a weight more than twice his body weight above his head! But he also needs fitness, speed, balance, gymnastic skill and, not least, courage. **Balance** is essential for him to use his strength and speed to the maximum, and to be in full control of the weights.

The weightlifter has to get the bar into positions that allow his strong leg and back muscles and hip joints to do most of the work of lifting. If he is not in balance when lifting, great stress is placed on parts of the body which are unable to cope with the forces needed. Stress can cause muscle strains and injuries to the back and abdomen.

The two hands snatch

Look at the drawings of a weightlifter doing the 'two hands snatch' [Fig. 3]. This is one of the Olympic lifts.

Fig. 1 A female bodybuilder

Fig. 2 The 'snatch'

  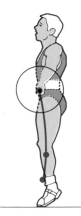  

1   See how the weightlifter has a straight back. His feet are firmly on the ground and his knees are bent close to the bar. As soon as he begins to lift the bar he has to take account of the centre of gravity of both the bar and his body.

2   He brings the bar towards his shins so that it is over the centre of his lifting base (i.e. his feet). The diagram also shows how the bar is moved towards the line which passes through the centre of gravity of the weightlifter.

3   When lifting the bar above his knees, he keeps his back straight. At the same time he extends his knees and pushes his hips upwards and towards the bar. He can produce his greatest lifting force in this position. The bar is lifted up and he squats down.

4   When the bar is above his head, and he is still squatting, he moves the bar back to bring it into line over his feet. The centres of gravity of his body and the weights are now directly over his feet.

5   In this balanced, stable position, the lifter can stand up straight to complete a perfect lift!

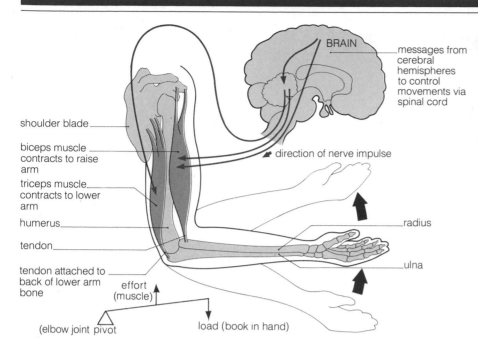

shoulder blade

biceps muscle contracts to raise arm

triceps muscle contracts to lower arm

humerus

tendon

tendon attached to back of lower arm bone

BRAIN

messages from cerebral hemispheres to control movements via spinal cord

direction of nerve impulse

radius

ulna

effort (muscle)

(elbow joint) pivot

load (book in hand)

Fig. 3 The weightlifter Mario Martinez

Fig. 4 Control of arm movement by the brain

Muscles at work

We do not all wish to be weightlifters but it is interesting to learn how muscles work. Look at the diagram of parts of the arm and connections to the brain [Fig. 4]. We use the diagram to explain three important processes in moving the arm.

Find the **biceps** and **triceps** muscles on the diagram. When you raise and bend your arm, the biceps contracts (gets shorter) and the triceps relaxes . When you lower and straighten your arm, the triceps contracts and the biceps relaxes. Control of the arm depends on the biceps and triceps muscles being **coordinated**. One muscle contracts as the other muscle relaxes.

Checking muscle power

There are some organs called **stretch receptors** inside the muscles. The stretch receptors are linked to the brain. So when a muscle is contracting or relaxing, the brain is informed so that it can control further movement.

A stretch receptor acts in a way similar to a speedometer in a motor car. The driver can see how his speed is changing and so adjust the force of his foot on the accelerator.

Controlling the muscles

The brain controls the muscles. Messages to the muscles from the brain are carried by cells called **neurones**. Neurones are long and thin and ideal for carrying tiny electrical signals called **impulses**. (Nerves are made up of many neurones.) When impulses in the neurones reach the muscles, they are made to contract.

Putting it all together

The human body is controlled by the brain. Thousands of signals are passing to each muscle in the body at any one time. We are unaware of these signals and run, walk and so on, quite naturally.

QUESTIONS

1 A weightlifter is in balance when the centres of gravity of the weights and his body are in a vertical line above his feet. Try to explain why he is likely to fall over if the centres of gravity are not in this line.

2 Would you like to be an Olympic weightlifter? Give reasons for your answer.

3 Where in the body are neurones and stretch receptors? What jobs do they do?

4 Why do you think at least two different muscles are needed to operate a limb? Name the two main muscles that raise and bend your arm.

5 Where does the energy come from which is needed for the muscles to work?

14 Chemicals for control

Many athletes had tried to run a mile in under four minutes. Roger Bannister was the first man to achieve it [Fig. 1]. News of his success was sent all round the world. In this chapter you can read the words of Roger Bannister as he tried to explain his feelings during the run.

Describing the last fifty yards, he said

'I had a moment of mixed joy and anguish, when my mind took over. It raced ahead of my body and drew it compellingly forward. I felt that the moment of a lifetime had come. There was no pain, only a great unity of movement and aim.

'I was driven on by a combination of fear and pride. My body had long since exhausted all its energy but it went on running just the same. This was the crucial moment when my legs were strong enough to carry me over the last few yards as they never could have done in previous years. With five yards to go, the finishing tape seemed almost to move away from me. Would I ever reach it? Those last few seconds seemed never-ending. The arms of the world were waiting to receive me if only I reached the tape without slackening my speed. If I faltered, the world would be a cold, forbidding place, because I had been so close. I leapt at the tape. My effort was over. I collapsed, almost unconscious.'

(From *We Were There* by Godfrey Caute)

The many complex body activities associated with running are co-ordinated and controlled by the nervous system. In *13 Muscle power* you can read how the brain, nerves, muscles and skeleton work together to ensure efficient movement. Bannister trained hard for this attempt on the world record. The physical preparation involved a great deal of hard work similar to that described in *15 A marathon*.

But the supreme effort made by Bannister required more than physical preparation. It needed physical endurance and the *will* to succeed. How did Roger Bannister gain the inner strength to drive him on?

My body had long since exhausted all its energy but it went on running all the same.

The help Bannister needed came from a natural chemical in his body called **adrenaline**. Adrenaline comes from the adrenal glands which are just above the kidneys. These glands release adrenaline into the bloodstream during times of stress or fear. Can you remember how you feel just before an important event like an exam or a race? Have you felt your heart beating faster, ringing in your ears, 'butterflies' in your tummy [Fig. 2], nervousness, a need to go to the toilet, a dry mouth, goose-flesh (pimples), shivering or a clammy feeling from sweating? These effects are usually due to adrenaline carrying 'messages' in the bloodstream to parts of the body. These feelings may cause you distress, but the adrenalin helps you to face difficult situations.

The total effect of adrenaline in the body is to prepare the body for 'fight-or-flight' situations. The body prepares itself to stand firm, defend itself, or to beat a hasty retreat.

. . . my mind took over. It raced ahead of my body and drew it compellingly forward. . . . There was no pain, only a great sense of unity of movement and aim.

Fig. 1 Roger Bannister breaking the four-minute mile in 1954

Fig. 2 Side effects of stress or fear

One of the most important effects of adrenaline is to raise the level of sugar in the blood. When adrenaline in the blood reaches the liver, it stimulates the breakdown of large molecules of glycogen stored there. The molecules of glycogen are broken down into small molecules of sugar. Sugar molecules are then carried by the blood to every cell in the body. The cells use the sugar to provide energy through respiration. This extra energy allows the cells to carry out their work at a greater rate.

Once the race is over, the danger past, the examination finished or the performance ended, the effects of adrenaline wear off. It is very important that these effects do wear off quickly because otherwise the body suffers from a lot of 'wear and tear'. It is also important for the body not to produce too much adrenaline. No one could keep up the tension needed to run a four-minute mile for long. Four minutes is long enough!

I leapt at the tape. My effort was over. I collapsed, almost unconscious.

Hormones in the body

Adrenaline is one of a group of substances in the body called **hormones**. Many important body activities are coordinated and controlled by the release of hormones directly into the blood. Hormones are released from **endocrine glands** [Fig. 3] in very small quantities by two processes: nerve impulses from the brain can trigger release of hormones from glands; hormones can also be released by the presence of other hormones. The blood carries hormones to all parts of the body. Hormones act as chemical messengers and cause various parts of the body to function in a certain way.

Each hormone produces a very specific effect on a particular group of cells or tissue or organ, and if the wrong amount of a hormone is produced, disorders may occur [Fig. 4]. Very few hormones produce effects on all parts of the body. The story about Roger Bannister shows that adrenaline is a hormone which produces many effects on the body.

Effects of adrenaline on the body

1. Pupils of eyes enlarge
2. Goose-flesh forms
3. Air passage tubes relax allowing increased air flow to lungs
4. Peristalsis stops—no food passes through alimentary canal
5. Digestion stops
6. Bladder contraction becomes difficult
7. Rate of heartbeat increases
8. Almost all blood vessels constrict
9. Blood pressure increases
10. Glycogen is converted to sugars in the liver
11. Mental awareness increases
12. Nerves and senses are set 'on edge'

Hormones help the brain to *control* the body. Electrical impulses are like electrical 'messengers' passing through the nervous system. When electrical messengers reach endocrine glands they cause the release of hormones which are like 'chemical messengers'. If a part of the body receives a message from the correct hormone it will act in the required way.

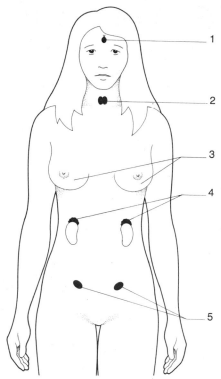

Fig. 3 The main endocrine glands of the body: 1 pituitary, 2 thyroid, 3 mammary (only in female), 4 adrenal, 5 ovaries (testes in males)

Fig. 4 Hormone imbalance causing goitre

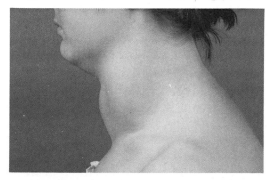

QUESTIONS
1. Describe something which made you feel frightened. Then describe what you felt your body doing.
2. What is the effect of adrenaline on glycogen and how does this help the body in times of stress?
3. Adrenaline is often called the 'fight and flight' hormone. What do you think this means?
4. Why is it important for the effects of adrenaline to wear off quickly? How do you think this happens?
5. Find out about two other hormones and the effects they produce in the body.

15 A marathon

The first marathon was run in Greece in 490 B.C. when a runner took news of a battle from Marathon to Athens.

Nowadays thousands of people run marathons each year. But each athlete has to prepare his or her mind and body to run over 26 miles in one go. In this chapter you can read about some of the preparations which these people make.

The purpose of training

Training is necessary to make the body work a little harder than it is used to. The marathon runner will train at a faster pace than he would run a marathon. Therefore if the body is trained to run faster than marathon pace it will be prepared to cope with the increased demands of the marathon. Generally marathon runners train using three distinct running speeds. Slow running helps to build up endurance and is often used as a recovery session between two harder sessions. A steady running pace develops speed and builds up the heart–lung system. Fast running sessions are used to improve the body's resistance to stress.

A good club runner begins to prepare for a marathon at least 3 months ahead. Plans include races, many hours of planned running at different speeds, and changes in diet.

During the training period the runner must eat a regular and balanced diet. The diet should include a lot of carbohydrates to supply the energy required in training.

The training schedule

In the early days, runners will cover 50 miles per week. 'Hard' days are usually followed by 'easy' days. The weekly total is increased every 2 to 3 weeks and at least two long runs per week are added. Different patterns of running are used. 'Interval running' is fast running over short distances followed by jogging slowly. The fast running increases the heart rate and jogging allows it to fall again. Jogging also helps to build up stamina. The pattern is repeated a set number of times. 'Repetition' training is the next stage. In this the runner covers set distances 'against the clock' with fixed periods to recover. Runners also run up hills to build up strength in the back, abdomen and thighs.

Fig. 1 The start of the London Marathon

Fig. 2 A drinks station

Fig. 3 Runners sponge themselves to keep cool during the race

Fig. 4 The finish: runners receive 'space blankets' to keep warm

Simple 'loosening up' exercises must be used before and after running. These exercises help the body to prepare for running and to return to normal afterwards. They increase the temperature of the muscles before running and help to prevent strains in muscles and tendons.

Final preparations

Two weeks before the marathon, the training programme is reduced. If 60 miles per week have been covered, this will be reduced to 40 miles and then to 20 miles in the final week. On the last two days there may be no running at all.

Some runners change their diet during the final week. The change in diet is to try and prevent the runner from 'hitting the wall'. This problem can be felt by a runner after about 20 miles of a race when he suddenly becomes very weak and his speed drops. It is caused by the body running out of **glycogen** which supplies energy. So one week before the race the athlete runs 20 miles to use up a lot of glycogen. Then for three days he eats only small quantities of carbohydrates. This seems to 'trick' the body into making more enzymes which cause glycogen to be produced. In the final three days before the race the athlete changes to a diet very high in carbohydrates. In this way, it is thought that the glycogen in the muscles and liver can be doubled up.

A training diary	
Sunday	13–16 miles slow to steady. Record time.
Monday	Warm up 1 mile. 5 miles good speed, untimed.
Tuesday	5–7 miles on grass, including 8 × 200 yds striding.
Wednesday	13 miles at marathon speed, starting slowly
Thursday	Long warm up. 6–8 miles Fartlek*
Friday	Rest or 3-mile jog
Saturday	Race or 2 × 3 miles repetition (5 mins recovery).

*Sprint, jog, walk sequence

Fig. 5 Example of a training programme during the tenth week of preparation

Fig. 6 A graduated race programme

	Several 5-mile races
Mid-March	10-mile race
End of March	10-mile race
Mid-April	10-mile race
Early May	15-mile race
Late May	20-mile race
Late June	**Marathon**

All races should be well spaced out to allow time for full recovery.

Race day

Breakfast should be eaten at least three hours before the race. Food which can be easily digested such as cereal, toast and scrambled egg is suitable, with as much fluid as possible. A further 250 cm³ at least of water should be drunk about half an hour before the race to keep up the body fluid levels.

Along the route runners can use the feeding stations placed about every 3 miles. They provide water, dilute fruit juice and special drinks. The rule is to drink little but often. Between feeding stations are sponging stations. Runners cool themselves by sponging down their faces, necks and thighs. Cooling the thighs is important because they produce a lot of heat. If this heat can be removed, muscle tightness and fatigue can be delayed.

Controlling body heat is a big problem for a marathon runner. About 20 times more heat is being produced during a marathon than when at rest. As much as 1 kg of fluid may be lost. If the weather is hot and humid, sweat will not evaporate and heat will build up in the body. This could produce overheating or **hyperthermia** and cause serious fatigue, dizziness and possible collapse.

After the race, the runner must keep warm by putting on a track suit or using a space blanket. Above all, the runner must keep moving, even slowly, to ward off stiffness. A lot of drink must be taken for 2 to 3 hours after a race, and a meal rich in carbohydrates is needed to restore energy reserves.

On the day after, a jog for a mile or so is advised. Then 2 to 3 miles is jogged on the following day, and so on. Jogging helps the body to move properly again and to remove waste products from the muscles. Soon all stiffness and weariness disappears and the runner is ready to prepare for the next race.

QUESTIONS

1 Why do runners take care about the quantity of carbohydrates they eat?
2 What is 'hitting the wall' and how do marathon runners try to avoid it?
3 Why is a hot and humid day bad for a marathon runner?
4 Why is it important to drink before, during and after a marathon?
5 How do space blankets help the runners after a marathon?

16 Keeping dry

How do you feel after climbing out of a swimming pool on a cool or windy day? You probably feel cold. You may shiver and rush to wrap a towel around you [Fig. 1]. Your body loses a lot of heat when wet. The same happens to other mammals and to birds. We must keep dry to keep warm.

In this chapter you can read about the problems of mammals and birds in keeping dry and warm. But first, it may help if you think about the reasons for keeping warm and why much heat is lost if the body is hot.

Body temperature

You will know that your body temperature stays at about 37°C. This is a higher temperature than that of the air in most parts of the world. Having a steady high body temperature allows us to inhabit places in the world with extreme climates. The same applies to other mammals and birds. But the price to be paid for a high steady body temperature is high. About 80% of the energy released from food is used in keeping up the body temperature. So mammals and birds cannot afford to lose a lot of heat.

Cooling by evaporation

Heat is lost from a wet surface through **evaporation**. This process requires heat to change the liquid water on the skin into water vapour which then diffuses into the atmosphere. Most of the energy required will be taken from heat in the body. So the body temperature drops. But when water evaporates from outer fur, feathers or clothing, most of the heat used will be taken from the air. So the body will hardly cool at all.

Fig. 1 It feels warmer in the water

Keeping ourselves dry and warm

Have you ever been running or played games on a cold wet day? If so, you may have put on damp clothing, such as a damp track suit, afterwards to keep warm. But this would probably not have helped. This is because damp clothing is a poor insulator of heat. Heat can pass 20 times more easily through water than through still, dry air! What you really need to keep warm is a layer of warm dry air next to the skin. In very cold temperatures or when it is windy, put on several layers of clothing to trap several layers of air. Wool clothing is very good for insulating the body against heat loss.

Have you ever used a sleeping bag? It is surprising how well a sleeping bag can keep you warm, even on a very cold night. The bag works well because of the still air which is trapped in the filling. Many kinds of filling materials are available to choose from. Fine duck feathers and down are suitable for Arctic weather. This filling is also very expensive! A synthetic filling can be used for normal summer camping. The thicker the filling, the warmer the sleeping bag will be. The filling should be

Fig. 2 A tent is made of waterproof material. The flysheet traps a layer of air and provides insulation

covered with fabric which is almost waterproof. But air must be able to pass through the fabric to allow your body to 'breathe'. This will enable moist air produced by the body during the night's sleep to escape into the atmosphere. In this way, the air trapped around you is kept dry and keeps you warm.

Tent material is often made of closely woven cotton fabric which has been waterproofed. This material is ideal as it allows the tent to 'breathe' whilst at the same time protecting it against wind, rain and cold. Most tents have an extra covering over them called a **flysheet** [Fig. 2]. This is usually made of a fully waterproof material such as terylene or nylon. The flysheet covers the whole tent and traps a layer of still air several centimetres thick between the inner tent and itself. This provides added protection as it helps make the tent draughtproof. It also keeps it cool in hot weather and warm in colder weather. This is precisely what hair on mammals and feathers on birds do.

Otters and seals must keep dry too

We can dress to suit the weather but most other mammals only have one set of clothing! However, they have special ways of keeping their skin dry and warm. The outer layer of skin is covered with dead cells made up of a waterproof substance called **keratin**. **Sebaceous glands** in the skin of mammals secrete oil onto the hairs. (Does your hair become 'greasy' if you do not wash it for a few days?) The oil helps to make the hairs waterproof and keeps them in good condition.

Aquatic mammals like otters and seals spend a lot of time swimming in very cold water [Fig. 3]. They have coats of dense fur next to the skin which trap a thin layer of still air. But this layer of air only insulates well if it is kept dry. So the outer hairs have to be waterproof. The otter has special outer hairs which overlap one another and prevent water from reaching the underfur.

How do birds stay dry?

Birds keep a steady body temperature of 41°C. So they need even better insulation than mammals. Most birds 'fluff out' their feathers in cold or windy weather. This provides a thicker layer of warm dry air between the skin and the outer feathers.

Herons and hawks have special 'powder-down' feathers. These feathers grow all the time and are never moulted. Instead, the tips of the feathers break down into a powder which is water resistant. The birds use the powder during preening to help keep their feathers waterproof.

Other birds obtain oil from a preen gland just above the tail [Fig. 4]. They first dampen their feathers and then rub the oil into them. Oiling the feathers makes them waterproof and helps to keep them good insulators. The air trapped inside them gives buoyancy to many water and sea birds.

Penguins do not lose their old feathers until the new ones are fully formed. The new feathers grow between the old ones. The penguin combs out the old feathers with its beak and feet. Keeping the old feathers avoids spaces in its coat through which body heat can escape. The feathers are also very oily and water repellent. You can read about penguins keeping warm in *17 Why do penguins have cold feet?*

Fig. 3 An otter

Fig. 4 A 'darter' taking oil from a gland to preen

QUESTIONS

1 Before you have an injection in your arm, the nurse usually rubs on ether. Ether evaporates very quickly. Explain why the ether makes your arm feel cold.

2 Seabirds are often found on the beach covered in oil from tankers. Their rescuers sometimes clean off the oil with detergent like washing-up liquid. Explain why the birds must not be released straight away after being cleaned in this way.

3 Why do you need to wrap up more on a windy day than on a calm day, even though the air temperature is the same?

4 Why should you keep your track suit dry when playing games on a cold and wet day?

5 Where in a mammal can you find keratin? Give one example of its value in keeping the body warm.

17 Why do penguins have cold feet?

All living organisms are adapted to survive in their environment. For example, fish have fins for swimming, birds have wings for flying and ducks have webbed feet for paddling. Many animals adapt their behaviour by migrating or hibernating when conditions become unfavourable. Plants are also adapted for their surroundings. For example, desert plants are able to obtain and store scarce water. Climbing plants cling and twine around other objects as they grow towards sunlight.

In this chapter, you can read about adaptations which help animals to keep their body temperature steady. First you can read about a penguin ('warm'-blooded or endothermic) and then about a crocodile ('cold'-blooded or ectothermic).

How do penguins keep warm?

Emperor penguins live in the harsh weather of Antarctica. Their body temperature of about 41°C is much higher than the temperature of their surroundings. So they must try to prevent loss of heat from their bodies.

A penguin's feathers trap a lot of still air. This still air cuts down heat loss because it is a very good **insulator**. Penguins are also insulated by a layer of fat or **blubber** beneath the skin. When penguins are in the water, their wet feathers are not as good at keeping them warm. It is the blubber which is their best insulator when wet.

Penguins have special ways of behaving when the temperature falls. When it falls to − 40°C and there are blizzard conditions, hundreds of penguins huddle together [Fig. 2]. They remain there without moving for days. A huddle saves energy because the penguins do not have to move around to keep warm. It also cuts down heat loss. This is because only about one-sixth of each bird's surface is exposed to the weather when huddling. The penguins take it in turns to be on the outside of the huddle. They also keep their backs to the storm. The huddle slowly moves round so that each part has a turn on the side of the storm.

The penguin 'heat exchanger'

Penguins have an unusual adaptation in their feet. Have you ever wondered if penguins have cold feet? After all, their feet are bare of feathers! Without feathers, their feet must get very cold and body heat must be lost through them.

Yes, penguins do have cold feet, but only a little body heat is lost through them. Penguins have a kind of heat exchanger! They are able to keep the temperature of their feet close to that of their surroundings.

The heat exchange system [Fig. 1] consists of a number of arteries and veins wrapped around each other. Under cold conditions, when body heat needs to be conserved, the veins near the surface of the feet constrict (become narrower). Most of the blood then flows in the veins in the

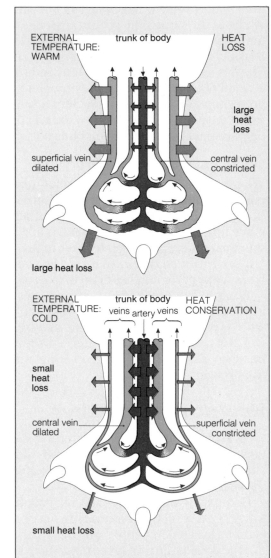

Fig. 1 A model of the simple heat exchange system in a penguin's foot

Fig. 2 Penguins in a huddle

Fig. 3 Nile crocodile basking in the sun

Fig. 4 Nile crocodile half submerged

middle of the feet. These veins lie parallel to the arteries. So when blood from the body flows down through the arteries and into the feet, it meets the cooler blood of the veins running up from the feet to the body. The blood in the arteries is able to transfer a large proportion of its body heat to the cooler blood of the veins. So blood returning to the body suffers only a small drop in temperature.

In warmer conditions the surface veins dilate (widen) and the deeper veins constrict. Therefore most of the blood in the arteries entering the feet passes into the veins close to the surface of the feet. In this way surplus heat can be lost from the feet.

Penguins can also lose heat by gently ruffling their feathers.

The Nile crocodile on the move

The Nile crocodile produces a small amount of body heat and its body is poorly insulated. Because of these features the crocodile depends on gaining heat from its surrounding warm environment. The crocodile follows a routine each day and moves back and forth between places in the sun, shade and water. In this way it can keep its body temperature close to 25°C at all times.

At dawn, the crocodile leaves the water in which it has spent the night. It basks for 2 to 3 hours in the sun on the sandy bank of a river, hardly moving and with its jaws wide open. Its body is slowly warmed up by the sun [Fig. 3].

By mid-morning the air temperature is higher than the water temperature. If the crocodile stayed in the sun, its body temperature would rise above 25°C. So it moves into the shade or back into the water. In the water, it usually stays half submerged [Fig. 4]. In this way, the heat its back absorbs from the sun is balanced by loss of heat through conduction from its body into the water.

The crocodile may sunbathe again in the afternoon, but at dusk it returns to the water. The fall in temperature of the night air is far greater than that of the water and also more rapid. So the crocodile avoids this sharp fall in temperature by returning to the water.

Thermoregulation

The crocodile has to keep moving around to keep its body temperature steady. It has to absorb energy from the sun when cool and to minimise heat loss from its body at night. This moving is called **behavioural thermoregulation**.

18 Computers and the brain

One of the most remarkable machines which has been developed in the last thirty years is the computer [Fig. 1]. Cars, televisions, washing machines, telephones, offices, machine assembly lines, even artificial heart pacemakers, increasingly depend upon computer systems. The computer acts as the 'brain' which enables machines or businesses to function efficiently. However, we must not think of the computer and the brain of an animal as similar structures. They are not. Even the simple brain of the earthworm is much more complex and sophisticated than most computers. The human brain has a work capacity equal to the combined efforts of *several million* computers.

Both the computer and the brain are able to deal with vast amounts of information rapidly and in a variety of different ways. In both cases the information which is fed into them is in the form of minute pulses of electricity. Here the major similarities end.

Computers are machines that perform *some* of the functions of the brain. They can make decisions rapidly, even faster than the human brain, but they cannot 'think' for themselves. They are primarily machines for doing arithmetic. This chapter is about some of the similarities and differences between computers and the brain.

Memory stores

Both the computer and the brain have vast **memory stores**. The memory of a computer has to be filled with information chosen by human operators. They can call up information, or **data**, from the computer's memory and use it as required.

The memory in the brain stores information collected by sense organs such as the eyes and ears. The part of the brain which stores information is called the **cortex**. The kind of information collected, and the time it is stored for, depend on the value of the information to the animal.

Input and Output

Information being fed into a computer [Fig. 2] is called **input** data. Data may be recorded, using a keyboard, onto punched cards or paper tape, or as typed information. The **output** from a computer is displayed on a VDU or on paper using a **line printer** [Fig. 3].

Information for the brain is collected by the senses. Output information is fed to muscles and other parts of the body. There is no need for the brain to give a printout of data because the data is immediately used by the body. Of course, some information is stored in the memory for use later.

Some computers *are* used to control equipment directly. You can read below about computers for robots.

Central processing unit

A computer needs a program to make it do useful work. But it also needs a **supervisor** program to tell it how to load and use programs. A supervisor program is permanently stored in the memory of the computer. The central processing unit (CPU) uses the supervisor

Fig. 1 A main frame computer

Fig. 2 Flow diagram showing the four major components in a computer system

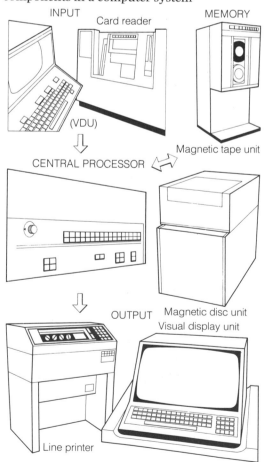

INPUT Card reader   MEMORY

(VDU)

CENTRAL PROCESSOR

Magnetic tape unit

OUTPUT   Magnetic disc unit
Visual display unit

Line printer

Fig. 3 Print-out of a computer program

```
  RP0808: NUMBER OF RECORDS IN TABLE=        64  LINES=      64
    FILE PVSTATS
      COMPUTE
      SET 1
      TYPELCC X10,1
      FORMO1 X2,2,X1,5,1,2,3,50,6,4,4
      ORDERO1 WNO,ACC,MODE,UNO,TIMET,BLT1,DEP,C,EDET
      TYPEO1 1
      FORMO2 X2,2,X1,5,1,2,3,X2,4,44,6,4,4
      ORDERO2 WNO,ACC,MODE,UNO,TIMET,ECT,BLT2,DEP,C,EDET
      TYPEO2 2
      LOG TYPE=REJECT,PVPERROR,NOMSG
      FILE PVSTATS

  DM0431: BLOCK       79 ASSIGNED AT RECORD       20

  DM0431: BLOCK       80 ASSIGNED AT RECORD      177
          RM0130: NUMBER OF RECORDS ENTERED=      294

  NO TRANSACTION ERRORS RECORDED
    FILE PVSTATS
      COMPUTE
      SET EC,EDEP
      KEY ONO,WNO,ACC
      FORM X2,2,X1,5,1,X5,2,4,X54,4
      ORDER WNO,ACC,MODE,UNO,EC,EDEP
      LOG TYPE=REJECT,PVPERROR,NOMSG
      FILE PVSTATS
          RM0130: NUMBER OF RECORDS ENTERED=       99

  ERROR/LOG       --ERROR COUNTS---      LOG COUNTS
    T Y P E       TRANS  RAW RECORDS     RAW RECORDS
    NOKE            47        NA            47
    COMP           148        NA           148
          294 RAW RECORDS WERE PROCESSED
    FILE PVPERRCR
```

program to carry out all the instructions in programs loaded into the computer.

The brain accepts signals from the sense organs and can automatically control muscles and other parts of the body. But we can *choose* to move parts of our bodies in different ways when we receive signals. For example if we see a wasp flying towards us we can hit it, or move sideways, or 'duck', or scream! Our brains must have a very complicated 'central processing unit' to let us do this. Computers can only 'do as they are told'. They can only make choices if we tell them exactly how to. But computers are becoming more 'intelligent'.

Robots

Do you remember learning to ride a bike? Are you learning to play a musical instrument? Both of these skills have to be 'taught' to the brain. The brain needs to know how to move parts of the body when we see, hear or feel a 'signal'. With enough 'practice' at the piano, for example, the brain will *automatically* make the fingers play the correct notes when the eyes see the 'music'.

Some robots [Fig. 4] work a little like this. You may have seen robots spraying paint on car bodies or furniture. An operator first moves the spray around correctly. The movements are stored as data in a computer memory. A program then uses the stored data to control the movement of the robot. The same movements can be repeated exactly as often as required.

Artificial intelligence

The most modern computers are becoming 'intelligent'. For example, they are able to understand speech, recognise objects and play with blocks of different shapes. They are beginning to develop in a similar way to babies and young children. These new computers show 'artificial intelligence'. Some new computers are called 'expert systems' because they can behave in a more human 'flexible' way. Instead of doing 'exactly what they are told', they can make guesses and take short cuts to solve problems.

You will soon see how these systems are able to help scientists, doctors and engineers.

Fig. 4 A robot on a car assembly line

QUESTIONS

1 Many new terms are used in describing computers. For each of these terms, describe what it means and how it is linked with computers: data, program, input, CPU, VDU, line printer.
2 Compare 'signals' used in computers with 'signals' used in the body.
3 Explain some ways in which new computers are becoming intelligent.
4 Robots seem to be taking over more and more jobs done by humans. What are the implications of this?
5 Explain what a binary digital code is. What other computer languages do you know? How do they differ from BASIC?

19 Kidneys–a moral problem

Your body cells are like minute chemical factories. The body cells need to be supplied with chemicals, and waste materials must be collected and taken away. The body cells must also be kept in a stable environment. For example, the pH and concentration of salt in the blood close to the cells must remain constant. Keeping a stable environment is called **homeostasis**.

Your kidneys play a vital part in keeping the body cells in a stable environment. The kidneys also help to remove waste products from the body. This chapter is about the kidneys and problems caused when they do not work correctly.

What do kidneys do?

Here are six tasks which kidneys do:

1 They remove waste containing nitrogen.
2 They maintain the blood at constant pH.
3 They control the concentration of salts in the blood.
4 They remove alcohol, drugs, hormones and other 'foreign' substances.
5 They remove surplus substances in the body.
6 They return glucose, amino acids and other essential substances to the body after blood has been cleaned.

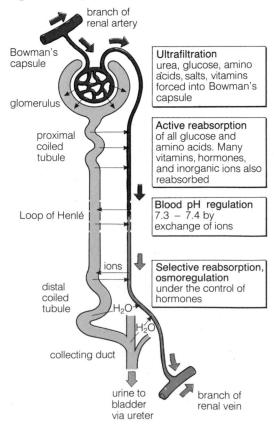

Fig. 1 Vertical section of a human kidney to show position of a single nephron

Labels: renal artery · renal vein · nephron (no blood supply shown) · pelvis · medulla · cortex · ureter · bladder

Inside a kidney

Look at the diagram of the section through a kidney [Fig. 1]. Fig. 2 shows the structure of a **nephron** and how it works. There are more than one million nephrons in a kidney. The nephrons carry out the six tasks listed above.

Kidney transplants

A diseased kidney can be replaced by a **kidney transplant**. Transplant operations are now quite common. The replacement kidney comes from a donor who has suddenly died, perhaps in a road accident. The biggest problem in a transplant operation is that the body will not accept any 'foreign bodies' placed inside it. To reduce the risk of rejection, the new kidney is 'matched' to the tissue of the body as closely as possible. Special drugs are used to stop the body from rejecting the new kidney. Unfortunately, the drugs also reduce the ability of the body to fight infections.

Kidney machines

If a kidney transplant is not possible, a kidney machine or **dialysis** machine can be used. The patient is connected to the machine through the radial artery in the patient's arm. Blood passes through the machine and back into the patient through the radial vein. A patient needs to spend two periods of about 12 hours each week on the machine [Fig. 3]. This gives you some idea of how much work your kidneys are doing!

Fig. 2 Urine production by a nephron

Labels: branch of renal artery · Bowman's capsule · glomerulus · proximal coiled tubule · Loop of Henlé · distal coiled tubule · collecting duct · ions · H_2O · urine to bladder via ureter · branch of renal vein

Ultrafiltration
urea, glucose, amino acids, salts, vitamins forced into Bowman's capsule

Active reabsorption
of all glucose and amino acids. Many vitamins, hormones, and inorganic ions also reabsorbed

Blood pH regulation
7.3 – 7.4 by exchange of ions

Selective reabsorption, osmoregulation
under the control of hormones

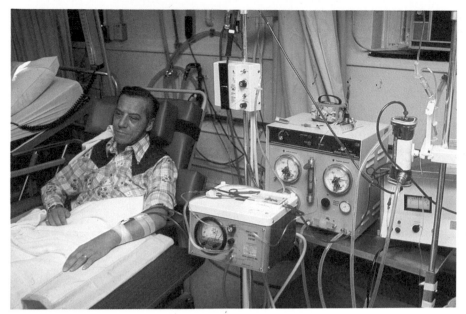

Fig. 3 Patient on a kidney machine

When blood first enters a kidney machine it is passed into a coiled cellophane tube. The cellophane is partially permeable so that salts, sugars, urea and many other substances leave the tube and pass into a liquid called the **dialyzate**. This liquid contains the normal concentrations of glucose and salts which are found in the blood. The dialyzate is pumped around the kidney machine and its composition is carefully controlled. In this way, the substances leaving or entering the blood can be controlled. The dialyzate must be changed regularly so that waste substances can be removed.

A moral problem

Healthy kidneys are in short supply and many patients need help. Without healthy kidneys, patients suffer and may die early. But kidney machines are expensive to run. It costs about £10 000 per year to run one kidney machine. There are too few kidney machines for all the patients who need one. Here are three ways which have been suggested of helping these people.

1 *Spend more money* It seems a simple solution to buy more kidney machines. But there are patients with other problems too. Should the country spend more on health? Would all taxpayers agree?
2 *Form a queue* Doctors in the United States have to choose which patients may use kidney machines. In a survey in 1984, doctors were shown to favour patients from certain backgrounds. Look at the list showing the order of preference. Someone must choose who uses the machine.
3 *Pay donors for a kidney* An American doctor has set up a company to buy kidneys from live donors. Healthy people have two kidneys but one is enough for good health. The doctor offers to pay about £3 500 for a kidney. Many people have objected to his plans on moral grounds. In his sales leaflets, he says, 'God gave us two kidneys and we only need one to live a normal healthy life. God gave us the intelligence and ability to perform kidney transplant operations. Giving financial compensation is 'the American way' of dealing with the shortage of donors.'

List of patients

In the queue for kidney treatment, this was the list – in order of preference – chosen by specialists and printed in the British Medical Journal.

55 year old woman with asthma
72 year old male vet
36 year old man with paraplegia
53 year old male diabetic
59 year old female diabetic
25 year old blind male diabetic
62 year old man with stroke
49 year old woman with rheumatoid arthritis
50 year old educationally subnormal woman
45 year old female analgesic abuser
67 year old Asian with no English
51 year old woman with breast cancer
50 year old man with ischaemic heart disease
30 year old man with schizophrenia
52 year old male alcoholic
29 year old hepatitis B positive man

QUESTIONS

1 Read the introduction again and find the word **homeostasis**. Explain what this means and then list the things which kidneys do to help in homeostasis.
2 Describe what blood *pH regulation* and *osmoregulation* mean.
3 Read again each of the ways in 'A moral problem' of helping those with diseased kidneys.
   For **1**, do you think that more money should be spent on kidney machines? Write out your arguments for what you think should be done.
   For **2**, look again at the list of (fictitious) patients. The list shows the order in which doctors would place these people in a queue for help on kidney machines. Comment on the list. Do you agree with the order? How would you arrange the list? Do you think that there should be a list at all?
   For **3**, do you think that the American doctor should be allowed to buy healthy kidneys? Give your reasons.

20 Developing a drug

Many of the developing countries of the world lie in semi-tropical or tropical regions. These have a rich and varied vegetation. For thousands of years the local people have used many species of plants for treating ailments and diseases.

Lately, developed countries have become interested in the use of herbal medicines. Medical science now accepts that many traditional medicines are successful in helping people to recover from injury and illness. Scientists are now trying to understand how some of these medicines succeed where modern medicine does not. In particular, scientists are studying the chemicals found in the plants used for the traditional medicines. It is essential that these plants are protected because of the medicines they may provide. This is one of the reasons that people are trying to stop the cutting down of the tropical rain forest in countries such as Brazil and the Philippines.

Some examples of plant extracts used in medicine

The well-known painkiller **morphine** was first obtained from opium poppies (*Papaver somniferum*) early in the nineteenth century. Even after intensive research and analysis, scientists have been unable to manufacture morphine synthetically in an economic way. They are still completely dependent on poppy plants for the drug. Unfortunately, many poppies are grown also to produce the drug heroin which is ruining the lives of millions of addicts around the world.

Quinine, which is used to treat malaria, is still extracted from the bark of the Cinchona tree in Peru. Heart problems were treated with an extract from the foxglove plant *Digitalis* [Fig. 1] long before the active ingredient, digitoxin, was synthesised from the foxglove in 1869. **Ephedrine** is an important drug which is used to increase the width of the air passage in the lungs. It was extracted from the Japanese ma huang plant (*Ephedra sinica*) in 1887. There are a number of different species of this plant around the world. For example traditional Chinese medicine uses *Ephedra* as a treatment for asthma.

Between 1965 and 1980, 25% of all prescriptions given out from chemists in the USA contained active ingredients which were still being extracted from plants.

The development of new drugs

The search for a new drug involves scientists from many branches of biological research. They include pharmacologists, physiologists, biochemists, microbiologists, surgeons and even specialists in electronics and photography. Major drug companies such as Beechams may spend tens of millions of pounds annually on research.

The development of a drug, from early research to selling the final product, may take between seven and ten years. Fig. 2 shows the stages involved in this development. First of all, a small project team states what properties are required of the drug and how they might be found. Then a number of substances are tested as candidates for the end product.

Fig. 1 The foxglove plant provides digitalis used to stimulate failing heart muscle

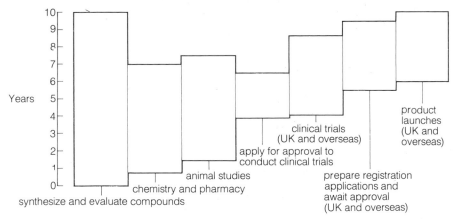

Years

synthesize and evaluate compounds

chemistry and pharmacy

animal studies

apply for approval to conduct clinical trials

clinical trials (UK and overseas)

prepare registration applications and await approval (UK and overseas)

product launches (UK and overseas)

Fig. 2 Typical stages in the development of a drug

When one substance has been selected, the scientists put together as much information as possible about the effect of the drug on normal and diseased tissues. They carry out extensive tests at the molecular, cellular, organ and organism level [Fig. 3]. It is essential that the scientists learn about any harmful effect the drug may have. They also need to know how the chemical composition of the drug changes when it is inside the body.

Clinical trials involve volunteers taking the drug and being checked for any harmful side effects, as well as beneficial effects for which the drug was developed. The newspaper cutting in Fig. 4 tells the story of a student who died whilst taking part in clinical trials of a new drug. It is not clear whether the drug was connected with his death, but the story does raise some important issues to think about. For example, are students, who are often short of money, being unfairly used by the drug companies for clinical trials? Are the regulations for clinical trials of new drugs strict enough?

Fig. 3 Scientists working in a drug company

Fig. 4 A tragedy during the trials of a drug

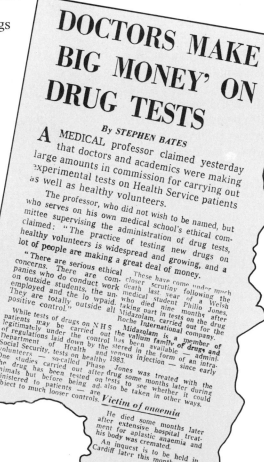

DOCTORS MAKE BIG MONEY' ON DRUG TESTS

By STEPHEN BATES

A MEDICAL professor claimed yesterday that doctors and academics were making large amounts in commission for carrying out experimental tests on Health Service patients as well as healthy volunteers.

The professor, who did not wish to be named, but who serves on his own medical school's ethical committee supervising the administration of drug tests, claimed: "The practice of testing new drugs on healthy volunteers is widespread and growing, and a lot of people are making a great deal of money.

"There are serious ethical concerns. There are companies who do conduct work on outside students, the unemployed and the low-paid. They are totally outside all positive control."

While tests of drugs on NHS patients may be carried out legitimately under the control of regulations laid down by the Department of Health and Social Security, tests on healthy volunteers — so-called Phase One studies carried out after the drug has been tested on animals but before being administered to patients — are subject to much looser controls.

These have come under much closer scrutiny following the death last year of a Welsh medical student Philip Jones, who died nine months after taking part in tests on the drug Midazolam, carried out for the Roche International company.

Midazolam is a member of the valium family of drugs and has been available — administered in the form of an intra-venous injection — since early 1983.

Jones was treated with the drug some months later during tests to see whether it could also be taken in other ways.

Victim of anaemia

He died some months later after extensive hospital treatment for aplastic anaemia and his body was cremated.

An inquest is to be held in Cardiff later this month.

QUESTIONS

1 There is great debate about using animals for testing new drugs. What are your views?

2 Explain in your own words why it may take up to ten years for a safe drug to be successfully developed.

3 Unfortunately today, many drugs used in medicine are also used illegally. Name three such drugs, their uses, and their effects when used improperly.

4 Do you think drug addiction is a serious problem? Discuss with your teacher how society should tackle the situation.

5 Why do you think that it is better to complete a course of medicine that has been prescribed, rather than stop taking the medicine as soon as you begin to feel better?

21 DNA and the genetic code

Have you ever wondered why cows give birth to cows and not to lions, and why lions give birth to lions and not to cows? The answer is not too surprising. It can be explained in terms of their parents. How this happened was a mystery until 1865, when Gregor Mendel did some plant breeding experiments in a monastery garden (read *23 Heredity, chance and change*). He was able to predict the appearance of the pea plants grown from a particular parent plant [Fig. 1]. He explained the results he obtained by 'particles' passing from parents to offspring. We now know that these 'particles' are what we call 'chromosomes'. The same principles apply to cows and lions.

Chromosomes

For the last hundred years, scientists have been studying cells and looking for ways in which information is passed on to offspring. We now know that every cell contains **chromosomes** in the nucleus. All human cells contain 46 chromosomes except for sex cells which contain 23. Chromosomes are tiny and can only be seen when the nucleus is dividing. They are made up of a string of **genes** which determine the characteristics of a person or other living thing. The genes are made of large complicated molecules called deoxyribonucleic acid, or **DNA** for short [Fig. 2]. The DNA molecules are surrounded by a thick coat of protein molecules for protection.

The structure of DNA

Scientists have known for many years that DNA makes exact copies of itself and carries coded instructions on how to make proteins. These proteins determine the characteristics of the individual.

But until 1953, no-one knew how DNA worked. In that year, two scientists called James Watson and Francis Crick discovered the structure of DNA. This was one of the most important discoveries in biology of the twentieth century because DNA holds the key to understanding how information is passed on to the next generation.

Watson and Crick had collected together a lot of information about DNA. For example, they knew that a molecule of DNA is made up of smaller molecules. These molecules include a sugar, phosphate, and molecules containing nitrogen called **bases**. There are four kinds of bases and they are known by their initial letters A, T, C and G. A scientist called Erwin Chargaff had also shown that DNA contains the same number of A molecules as T molecules and the same number of C molecules as G molecules.

Characteristics studied
dominant character × recessive character

stem length

tall stem
dwarf stem

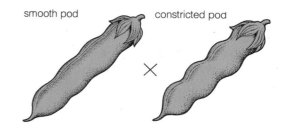

shape of pod

smooth pod
constricted pod

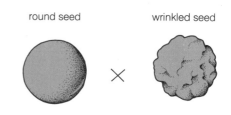

shape of seed

round seed
wrinkled seed

Fig. 1 Some of the characteristics of pea plants investigated by Mendel in his experiments

Fig. 2 Chromosomes are made up of genes which are made of molecules of DNA

typical human cell

nucleus
containing 46
chromosomes

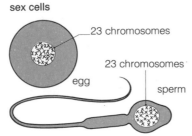

sex cells

23 chromosomes

23 chromosomes

egg

sperm

single chromosome

three genes

coiled DNA

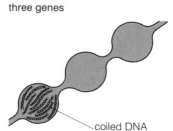

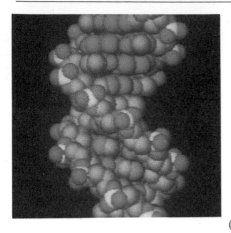

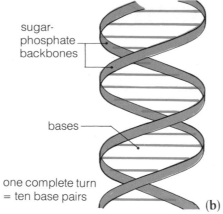

(a)

sugar-
phosphate
backbones

bases

one complete turn
= ten base pairs

(b)

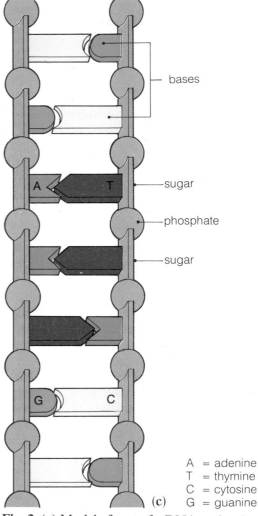

bases

sugar

phosphate

sugar

A = adenine
T = thymine
C = cytosine
G = guanine

(c)

Fig. 3 (a) Model of part of a DNA molecule (b) chains of molecules twisted round each other (c) the untwisted structure of a DNA molecule

Watson and Crick also knew of the results of Rosy Franklin and Maurice Wilkins who studied DNA with X-rays. They had shown that DNA has a 'regular' shape and is made up of repeated groups of similar molecules.

So Watson and Crick put all this information together and thought carefully about a possible structure for DNA. They suggested the famous 'double helix' structure in 1953. Look at the photograph of a model of this structure [Fig. 3a]. They suggested that each molecule of DNA has two long chains of atoms twisted round each other [Fig. 3(b)]. Each chain has a 'backbone' made up of millions of sugar and phosphate molecules arranged alternately. Sticking out at right angles from each sugar molecule is a base. An A base of one chain is joined to a T base of the other chain. Also a C base of one chain is joined to a G base of another chain. The order of these 'base pairs' is very important, as we shall discover later.

In 1962, Watson, Crick and Wilkins shared the Nobel Prize for Medicine for their work. Sadly, Rosy Franklin, who had done many experiments on DNA with X-rays, died before the Nobel Prize was awarded. She would probably have shared the prize had she lived.

How does DNA carry instructions?

You will remember that a chromosome consists of a string of genes (made of DNA) which decide a person's characteristics. How do they do this?

Francis Crick discovered that the arrangement of bases in one of the DNA chains of the double helix forms a **code**. This code determines the proteins that are made by a cell, which in turn determines the characteristics of that cell and the whole individual.

This is how the code works. Each group of *three bases* on a DNA chain represents a particular **amino acid**. Amino acids are the building blocks of proteins. So a length of DNA 300 bases long would carry instructions for 100 amino acids to be joined together. This sequence of amino acids will form a specific protein. A different sequence of bases would produce different amino acids and a different protein. So the sequence of bases for producing say, ginger hair is different from the order that produces blond hair, and so on.

It is now known that *each* gene carries the code for *one* protein or part of a protein.

The sequences of bases for all amino acids are known; this is called the **genetic code**. Cracking this code has helped other scientists to understand how proteins are made. This process is described in *22 Building proteins*.

QUESTIONS

1 Describe the structure of DNA in your own words. Illustrate your answer with a simple diagram.
2 What is the genetic code? Why is it so important?
3 Find out the number of chromosomes in the cells of two species of plants and two species of animals other than humans.
4 Using the information in this Chapter and *22* describe how the information carried by DNA is converted into the formation of a protein.
5 All human body cells contain 46 chromosomes, but our sex cells contain 23. Can you give a reason for this?

22 Building proteins

Proteins are found in every cell in every living thing. Without proteins, animals and plants would fail to grow and would quickly die. For example, proteins form **structures** such as muscle, hair, and cell membranes. They also speed up biological reactions as **enzymes** and defend the body against infection as **antibodies**.

The structure of protein

In living things there are large numbers of different protein molecules. Each protein molecule is made up of smaller molecules called **amino acids**. There are only 20 different kinds of amino acids in nature.

Amino acids form an 'alphabet' for making proteins. Just as there are thousands of different words in English made up of 26 letters, so there are thousands of different proteins made up of 20 amino acids. The average word has about 8 letters but the average protein molecule has several thousand amino acids.

Amino acids are also more complicated than words in another way. Words can only be 'understood' if written down in two dimensions [Fig. 1]. This is because a word is made up of letters in a special order. For example, the words LEFT and FELT are made up of the *same* letters but in a *different order* and mean quite different things. So it is with proteins, but they must be made up of amino acids arranged correctly in *three* dimensions.

Each amino acid contains the elements carbon, hydrogen, oxygen, and nitrogen. Some amino acids also contain sulphur. The chemical bonds which join one amino acid to the next in a protein molecule are called **peptide bonds**.

A 'protein factory'

Humans can make ten of the amino acids but the other ten can only be made by plants. This is one reason why all animals depend in the end on plants as their source of food. Animals obtain protein by eating plants or other animals and this protein is broken down into amino acids during digestion. The amino acids are absorbed into the blood and taken to cells all around the body. Once inside a cell, amino acids are joined together in a special way to make proteins.

You read above that amino acids are like the letters in a word and a protein is like the word itself. Inside the cell there are instructions on how the amino acids are to be put together to make the required protein. The instructions are in the code of the DNA molecules in the cell. Amino acids are placed in the correct order determined by the sequence of **bases** in a DNA molecule. You can read about how bases do this in *21 DNA and the genetic code*.

To follow how proteins are built from instructions in DNA molecules it might help to think about a car factory [Figs. 3–4].

Car designers draw detailed plans of how the parts of a car must be put together and in what order. This is just what the DNA molecule does

Fig. 1 Words are two-dimensional, proteins are three-dimensional

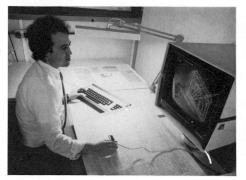
Fig. 2 A draughtsman's office

Fig. 3 A car assembly line

Fig. 4 The finished product

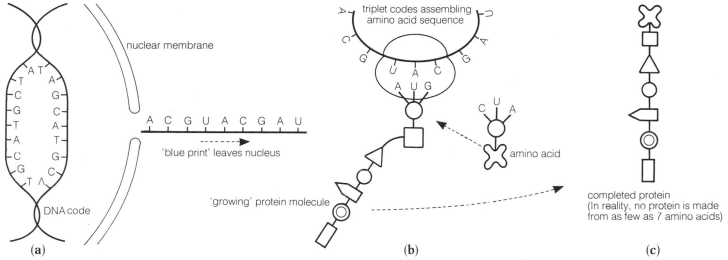

(a)

nuclear membrane

A C G U A C G A U

'blue print' leaves nucleus

DNA code

triplet codes assembling amino acid sequence

'growing' protein molecule

amino acid

(b)

completed protein
(In reality, no protein is made from as few as 7 amino acids)

(c)

Fig. 5 Making a protein (a) DNA determines the amino acid sequences (b) Amino acid chain assembled on the ribosome (c) Amino acid sequence in a protein. Notice the similarities between manufacturing a car and manufacturing a protein

Fig. 6 Rolls Royce

Fig. 7 Tractor

[Fig. 5]. It 'states' which amino acids will be in the protein and the order in which they will be joined. In building cars, copies of the plans are sent to the assembly plant. The assembly workers must then follow the plans and put the car parts together in the correct order.

There are many different 'models' of car. Each has the same kind of parts such as wheels, a gearbox and so on. But each model is different and depends on the actual parts used. So it is with proteins. It depends which amino acids are used and in what order they are joined together.

Look at the two vehicles in Figs. 6 and 7. They both have wheels, doors and so on, but they are quite different. This is because their parts are different and they are assembled differently. Proteins also have many different structures although they are all made from amino acids. Each protein has a different task to do.

QUESTIONS

1 What chemical elements combine together to form a protein? Now work out where and in what form plants take in these elements to make their own proteins.
2 Think of an example other than the car factory and explain how your 'model' is similar to how the cell makes a protein.
3 How do amino acids arrive in the cells of an animal?
4 What do you think would happen if the assembly of a protein was faulty? Ask your teacher to tell you about **mutations**.
5 Nowadays scientists can manipulate and alter some genetic instructions in cells. This is called **genetic engineering**. What are the dangers and advantages of this?

23 Heredity, chance and change

Do you look like either of your parents? Do your friends look like their parents? Tall parents often have tall children. The colour of eyes and skin, the shape of the nose, the kind of hair and other features are often inherited from parents [Fig. 1]. Such features are called **characteristics**.

Characteristics are passed on from generation to generation by the sex cells or **gametes**. The study of how characteristics are passed on is called **heredity**. This chapter is about the passing on of characteristics by animals and plants which reproduce by sexual reproduction.

Fig. 1 It's easy to see that these are members of the same family!

What do peas and humans have in common?

Gregor Mendel (1822–1884) carried out a long series of experiments on pea plants. He studied how characteristics, such as the length of stem, seed shape and flower colour, were passed on to new generations. He always used 'pure breeding' parent plants. These are plants which produce offspring identical to themselves if 'crossed' (bred) with other pure breeding plants with the same characteristics.

Look at Fig. 2 which shows the results of one of Mendel's experiments. A tall stem parent plant was crossed with a short stem parent plant. The first generation of plants from the seeds of the parents *were all tall*. This happened even though one parent was short. The first generation of pure breeding plants are called F_1 **hybrids**. (You can read more about hybrids in *24 Hybrids*.)

The F_1 plants were then crossed and the second generation plants were examined. Three quarters of the second generation were tall and one quarter were short. The second generation of pure breeding plants are called F_2 **hybrids**.

Mendel concluded from this experiment that tallness is a stronger characteristic in peas than shortness. He wrote that tallness is a **dominant** characteristic and shortness is a **recessive** characteristic.

Mendel published his results in 1865 and so began the branch of biology now called **genetics**. Scientists have discovered many other facts and Mendel's experiments are now explained as follows:

1 Gametes (sex cells) carry the **factors** which cause characteristics to be inherited.
2 These factors are parts of **chromosomes** which carry coded information.
3 Each part of a chromosome is called a **gene**.
4 Each characteristic is controlled by two genes, one of which is inherited from each parent.
5 The genes may be either **dominant** or **recessive**.
6 Each gamete carries only half the number of genes found in all other cells in the animal or plant.

(You can read more about chromosomes in *21 DNA and the genetic code*)

Many of the discoveries found by Mendel are similar to those found from studies of heredity in humans.

Fig. 2 Mendel's pea experiment

Parents

tall   short

First generation

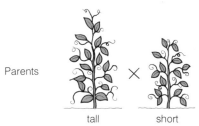

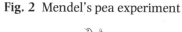
all tall

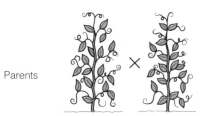

Parents

Second generation

all tall   short

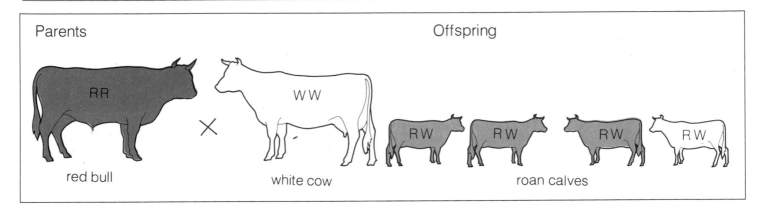

Parents — Offspring

red bull × white cow — roan calves

Fig. 3 Red hair Shorthorn bulls and white hair Shorthorn cattle produce calves with roan hair

Does inheritance always work this way?

Not all of Mendel's statements always work. Look at the Fig. 3 showing the offspring of a red hair Shorthorn bull and and white hair Shorthorn cow. All the calves have a mixture of red and white hairs! The calves are called **roan** calves. This is an example of **incomplete dominance**. The genes for red hair and white hair are equally dominant and both kinds of hair appear in the offspring. Here is another way of thinking about the result:

The red hair bull carries two identical red hair genes labelled 'RR'. The white hair cow carries two identical white hair genes labelled 'WW'.

(Look at the Fig. 3 again and note the letters.) Each parent carries two identical genes and so is called **homozygous**. But the roan hair calves contain two different genes, labelled 'RW': the R gene is inherited from the bull and W gene from the cow. The calves are called **heterozygous**. (In Greek, 'homos' means 'same' and 'heteros' means 'other'.)
   Animals or plants which have identical genes, and so are homozygous, are called 'pure-breeding' or 'pure strains'. Animals or plants which are heterozygous are called 'hybrids'.

Why are we all different?

You are unique and your friends are unique. No two human beings are exactly alike. Even 'identical' twins show slight differences. Here are three reasons why each person is unique:

1 Each person inherits a set of genes from each parent. Each set of genes in unique because it is taken from the hundreds of thousands of genes in the chromosome. All these genes are shuffled together when gametes are formed. So no two gametes are identical.
2 When male and female gametes join together at fertilisation, new combinations of genes are brought together for each offspring.
3 The appearance of an adult depends on the environment as well as on inherited genes. For example, a person who does not have an adequate and balanced diet will not reach the maximum height allowed by the genes. Even identical twins are slightly different although they have identical sets of genes.

Look around you at the variation between different kinds of trees. And the variation between trees of the same species. It is the variation between plants and between animals which adds to the beauty of the living world.
   You can read more about heredity in *24 Hybrids*.

QUESTIONS

1 Explain the meaning of *gametes* and *heredity*.
2 Write in your own words the conclusion of Mendel's experiment to show the meaning of *dominant* and *recessive* characteristics.
3 Explain the meaning of homozygous and heterozygous. Which of these terms is the correct description of the parent shorthorn bull and cow? Which is the correct term for the parent pea plants used by Mendel?
4 Why do 'identical' twins have differences?

24 Hybrids

Throughout the course of history, humans have struggled with the problem of providing enough food for themselves and their families. Hundreds of millions of people are still short of food today. One way of trying to produce more food is to use our knowledge of **genetics**. By breeding new varieties of plants and animals it is possible to provide more and better food.

In the last thirty years new breeds of animals and varieties of plants have been developed. They show rapid growth and produce high yields, even when raised in less than perfect conditions. A good example is the new varieties of wheat.

Wheat

Wheat is the most widely cultivated plant on Earth. Our modern wheat plants which are used to make flour came originally from wild plants. But over the last 4000 years, farmers have selected the finest plants to produce **hybrid** plants with better qualities. These qualities include early germination, resistance to cold and disease, rapid and sturdy growth, larger ear and grain sizes, increased protein content and improved baking qualities.

Recently, a hybrid cereal called *Triticale* was produced by crossing wheat (*Triticum*) with rye (*Secale*). The hybrid has many of the advantages of both parents. For example, *Triticale* has the hardiness and protein content of rye but gives a higher yield than wheat. Improved varieties of *Triticale* are being produced all the time using the methods described below.

Fig. 1 Different varieties of wheat are grown in the same conditions to compare growth

Hybridisation

Hybrids are plants or animals which have been reared from specially selected parents. Each parent is selected because it shows a special characteristic which is needed by the offspring. A parent must also be **pure breeding** for the characteristic. This means that the parent must always produce offspring with this characteristic when mated or crossed with another parent which has the same characteristic. In hybridisation, the following steps are taken in producing offspring. (The steps are described with animals but also apply to plant breeding.)

1 Cross male and female parents which both show *one* of the required characteristics. If the male and female offspring show the same characteristic, use these as parents to produce another generation of offspring. If all of this generation show the characteristic, the parents and offspring can be used as pure-breeding stock.
2 Repeat Step 1 using male and female parents which show a different required characteristic. In this way, another pure-breeding stock is obtained.
3 One animal is taken from each of the pure-breeding stocks in 1 and 2. The animals are crossed and become the parents for offspring called F_1 **hybrids**. These offspring will have the required characteristics from *both* parents.

Fig. 2 Breeders can choose the characteristics they want in an animal!

Look at Fig. 2 which gives an example of hybridisation. The parent on the left has the required characteristics A and C. The parent on the right has the required characteristics B and D. If the parents are from pure-breeding stock, the F_1 hybrid offspring will have all four of the required characteristics A, B, C and D.

Hybridisation-'plus'

In some cases of hybridisation, the offspring have characteristics shown by neither parent. For example, if a Large White boar is crossed with a Landrace sow, the piglets are heavier than their parents when they grow to full size. The production of offspring with improved characteristics is called **hybrid vigour**.

Hybridisation in action

Maize

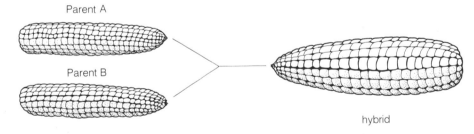

Parent A

Parent B

hybrid

The sweet corn cobs that we eat covered in butter are the fruits of F_1 hybrids. Look at Fig. 3 which shows that the cobs of F_1 hybrids are much bigger than the cobs of their parents. The grain yield can be increased by 250% by special breeding. This increase is due to hybrid vigour.

Chickens

A lot of research on the breeding of chickens took place during the Second World War when food was short in Britain. Some breeds, with light bones, have little muscle tissue. Most of their food is used up in producing lots of high quality eggs. Other breeds grow rapidly and produce a lot of muscle tissue. These breeds are used for meat production.

All of these special breeds are **hybrids**. They show better characteristics than either of their parents. This is another example of hybrid vigour.

Hybrid vigour

The appearance of many desirable characteristics in F_1 hybrids can be explained as follows:

1 The majority of desirable characteristics are controlled by dominant genes.

2 A pure-breeding parent possesses two dominant genes for the desirable characteristic.

3 Crossing two 'pure-breeding' parents ensures that a dominant gene for each desirable characteristic will be present in the F_1 hybrid.

4 Therefore, F_1 hybrids are heterozygous (see *23 Heredity, chance and change*) for all desirable characteristics, as shown in Fig. 2.

If two of the hybrids produced in Fig. 2 are used as parents, their offspring will show a complete range of characteristics. For this reason the seeds of F_1 hybrid plants are not usually sown. F_1 hybrids must always be specially bred from pure-breeding parents. This process is very expensive. However, the advantages of using F_1 hybrids in terms of improved yield, increased resistance to disease, etc. are so great that it is much more profitable to use them than either of the parental types.

Fig. 3 You can see that the F_1 hybrid cob is larger than either of the parents

QUESTIONS

1 Give two good reasons why hybridisation of plants or animals can be useful.
2 What steps must be taken to make sure that stock are pure-breeding stock?
3 What is an F_1 hybrid?
4 What 'plus' is obtained by crossing a Large White boar with a Landrace sow? What term is used to describe this 'plus'? Give two examples of plants which show this 'plus'.
5 Experiments have been carried out on mating animals of different species such as a sheep and a goat. Do you agree with these experiments? Give your reasons.

25 Acid rain

Rain falling over most of the Earth is slightly acidic. In some parts of Europe and North America, rain is often quite strongly acidic. It is then called **acid rain**. Power stations and factories are often blamed for acid rain. Gases are produced when fuels are burned and some of these dissolve in rain to form acids.

When acid rain falls on the ground, it slowly poisons the countryside [Fig. 1]. If rain is very acidic, it can kill fish in lakes, affect the growth of plants and poison drinking water. It is possible to reduce the acidity of rain and so protect the countryside, but it costs a lot of money. Is it worth the cost? Read about the problems and solutions and make up your own mind.

The cause of acid rain

Rain is normally slightly acidic with a pH of between 5 and 6. (The pH of a neutral liquid is 7.) This acidity comes from small amounts of gases in the atmosphere which dissolve in rain as it falls. Two of these gases are **sulphur dioxide** and **nitrogen dioxide**. Both gases are very soluble in water and become oxidised to form **sulphuric acid** and **nitric acid**.

Fig. 1 Death and damage caused by acid rain

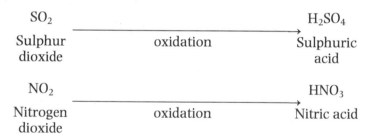

$$SO_2 \xrightarrow{\quad\text{oxidation}\quad} H_2SO_4$$
Sulphur dioxide — Sulphuric acid

$$NO_2 \xrightarrow{\quad\text{oxidation}\quad} HNO_3$$
Nitrogen dioxide — Nitric acid

Rain in parts of Europe and North America often has a pH of between 4 and 5. The pH has dropped to 3 in some areas. The high acidity is probably due to large amounts of sulphur dioxide in the atmosphere. Some 30 million tonnes of sulphur dioxide reach the atmosphere over Europe every year. About 90 per cent comes from the burning of oil and coal in power stations and 10 per cent from factories. Sulphur dioxide comes from compounds of sulphur in the fuels being burned. The graph in Fig. 2 shows how the quantity of sulphur dioxide in the atmosphere has increased with time.

What happens when acid rain falls?

Two main problems have been linked with acid rain. Firstly, freshwater lakes have become more acidic. And, secondly, new compounds of aluminium, cadmium, mercury and lead have been formed in the ground. These new compounds have been washed out of the soil into streams and down into lakes.

Strange changes occurred in Swedish lakes in the 1950s and '60s. Some lakes became very clear and changed to a beautiful blue colour. But almost all plants and animals died. Scientists tested the water and found a pH of 4·5. They then collected layers of mud from the beds of lakes which had been built up over thousands of years. The scientists

Fig. 2 Graph showing the increase in sulphur dioxide in the atmosphere between 1850 and 1970

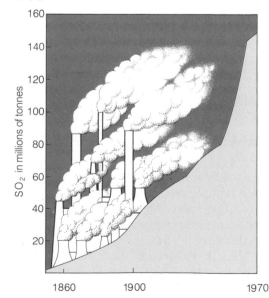

tested dead algae for pH in each layer. The pH at the end of the last Ice Age was about 7. It then fell steadily to about 6 and stayed at that value. But the pH suddenly fell to below 5 around 1950.

A big fall in pH like this causes serious changes to the life of a lake. The number of algae decreases rapidly as the pH falls below 6. Only a few species can survive. Animal plankton such as crustaceans are also affected. In most acid lakes, most animal plankton belong to only one species.

White mosses thrive in acid water below a pH of 6. As lakes became clearer, more sunlight reached below the surface. Some mosses could then grow in areas which were too dark before. Some plants, such as *Lobelia* and *Litorella* which grow on lake beds became overgrown with white mosses and green algae.

Insects and animals need food to live, and so are affected by changes to algae, animal plankton and plants. Falling pH values also affect them directly. Leeches, crustaceans and molluscs are affected at a pH of 6. One problem is that they can no longer use calcium to form shells. But one species of mayfly can exist until the pH reaches 5·4.

The first fish to suffer are roach, minnow and salmon, but pike and perch can survive until the pH reaches 5. Roach cannot reproduce so no young fish can replace the older generation. Aluminium compounds form a precipitate on the gills of all fish. The gills are damaged and cannot absorb enough oxygen into the blood.

Birds which feed on insects, larvae and fish are affected in turn as lakes become acidic. Their supply of food decreases, and poisonous compounds of mercury, cadmium and aluminium in their food and drinking water lead to other problems.

How can acid rain be prevented?

The main cause of acid rain is probably sulphur dioxide in the atmosphere. If the amount of sulphur dioxide from power stations burning oil and coal could be reduced, acid rain might be prevented [Fig. 3]. This could be done by removing sulphur compounds from fuels or by removing sulphur dioxide from the gases leaving power stations. Both methods are now being tried out. The cost of either method could mean an increase of between 2 and 5 per cent on all electricity bills. A typical home spends about £300 per year on electricity. The cost could rise by £15 to pay for removing sulphur dioxide.

Producers of electricity do not agree that removing sulphur dioxide would solve the problem of acid rain. The chemistry of acid rain is very complicated and a cheaper solution may be possible. Research is being carried out on this. In the meantime, **lime**, which is an alkali, is being added to lakes to **neutralise** the water. This is costly and has to be repeated every few years.

An international problem

Most of the gases from the chimneys of power stations and factories rise into the atmosphere and dissolve in water droplets. The gases may travel thousands of kilometres before reaching the ground in acid rain. The societies for the Conservation of Nature in Norway and Sweden claim that 9 per cent of the sulphur dioxide falling in acid rain on their countries comes from chimneys in Britain.

It is not easy to persuade people in one country to spend a lot of money so that the countryside in another country can be saved. Would you be willing to pay more for electricity to help the countryside in Sweden?

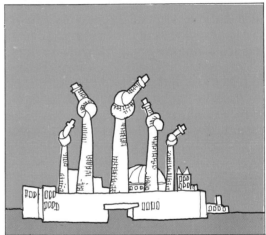

Fig. 3 A way must be found to prevent acid rain·

QUESTIONS

1 Use the graph in Fig. 2 to describe changes in the quantity of sulphur dioxide in the atmosphere over the last hundred years.
2 Why does the average age of fish in a lake increase as the lake becomes more acidic?
3 Why is lime sometimes added to lakes? Use the terms pH, acid, alkali and neutralisation in your answer.
4 Assume that power stations are the real cause of acid rain. Do you think that we should pay more for electricity to save the countryside in other countries? Explain why you think this way.
5 Organise a class debate on the motion:
'That the countries responsible for producing the gases that cause the acid rain should pay compensation to those countries affected by the acid rain'.

26 Life in the sea

Our knowledge of life in the sea is still very slight. It is only in the last 40 years or so that serious research has taken place. But even now, we know little more about the depths of the oceans than the surface of the moon. This chapter is about some of the plants and animals in the sea and how their lives are linked together. We shall see that the sea is a huge **ecosystem** in which each plant and animal plays its part. You can read about another ecosystem in *27 Life in the jungle*.

The source of life in the sea

Life in the sea depends on **photosynthesis** (see *1 Photosynthesis*). This is a process which involves the green chemical **chlorophyll** in plants. This chemical absorbs sunlight, and produces food in the presence of carbon dioxide gas and water. Photosynthesis is assisted by minerals such as nitrates and phosphates. So life in the sea begins with plants. Find Box 1 in the flow diagram about phytoplankton which are the small plants which produce food. Follow the other lines in numerical order to find your way around the 'web of life' in the sea.

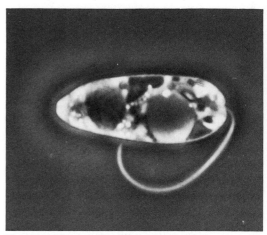

Fig. 1 A marine flagellate (× 200)

The web of life in the sea

1 Phytoplankton

This is a group of tiny plants including many that cannot be seen without a microscope. They contain **chlorophyll** which they use to produce food. Phytoplankton have been called the 'grass of the sea' because, like grass, they produce huge quantities of food for animals. Without phytoplankton no animals could survive in the sea. Because they need sunlight to produce food, phytoplankton live in the top 100 metres of the sea. Here are examples of two groups of phytoplankton:

Diatoms: They have diameters between $\frac{1}{10}$ mm and $\frac{1}{100}$ mm. They reproduce by splitting into two parts. This process is called **fission**. Fission takes place so rapidly that a single diatom may have 100 million descendants within one month!

Flagellates: They can move around using flagella or whips. Their name comes from the Latin word 'flagellum' meaning 'whip'. Can you see the flagellum in Fig. 1?

2 Zooplankton: the smaller animals.

Phytoplankton are eaten by **zooplankton**. These are tiny animals including many which are the young of lobsters, crabs and shrimps. Others remain small such as the **Foraminifera** which have shells. When they die, the shells fall to the bed of the ocean, and may collect in huge deposits. One such deposit formed the white cliffs of Dover. The cliffs are made of the calcium carbonate from foraminiferan shells deposited when the area lay below the sea.

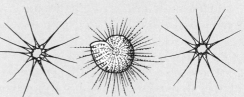

3 Krill: food for whales

Krill are large crustaceans and feed on zooplankton. Krill are a very important link in the food chain of the sea, because they are food for fish and whales.

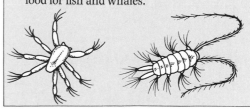

4 Crustaceans: are the largest group of zooplankton. They range in size from $\frac{1}{2}$ mm to 3 cm and are probably the world's biggest eaters. They can eat half their own weight of phytoplankton every day!

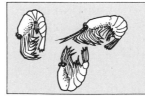

Creatures of the deep

Creatures have been found at the lowest depths. Some rise to the surface every day for food. Many are eaten by predators who wait for them to pass through their level of water. Others are able to survive at the very bottom. They feed on the remains of dead animals which fall to the bottom. Look at Figs. 2 and 3, photographs of creatures found at large depths.

Fig. 2 An angler fish with a luminous 'lure'

Fig. 3 A gulper eel with elongated jaws

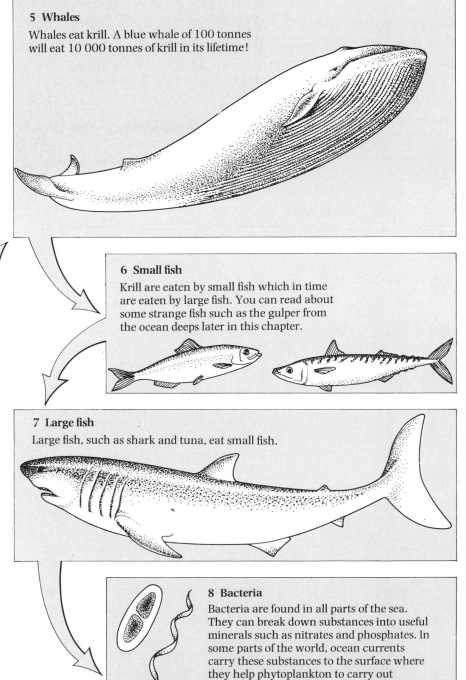

5 Whales

Whales eat krill. A blue whale of 100 tonnes will eat 10 000 tonnes of krill in its lifetime!

6 Small fish

Krill are eaten by small fish which in time are eaten by large fish. You can read about some strange fish such as the gulper from the ocean deeps later in this chapter.

7 Large fish

Large fish, such as shark and tuna, eat small fish.

8 Bacteria

Bacteria are found in all parts of the sea. They can break down substances into useful minerals such as nitrates and phosphates. In some parts of the world, ocean currents carry these substances to the surface where they help phytoplankton to carry out photosynthesis. So bacteria link the 'higher' members of the food web back to the phytoplankton which are the food producers.

QUESTIONS

1 Which creatures are described as the 'world's biggest eaters'? Why?
2 Draw a food chain to show the link between the following: krill, phytoplankton, foraminifera, whale.
3 In a different colour, add to your food chain the following: shark, gulper, bacteria. You have now made a food web. Why do you think the term *web* is used?
4 The word *ecosystem* is used to describe the sea. In an ecosystem, each plant and animal plays its part. Explain why the sea is described as an ecosystem.
5 What would happen to life in the sea if sunlight ceased to penetrate the water? How would these changes occur?

27 Life in the jungle

How do you imagine a jungle? Do you think of huge apes swinging from trees, Tarzan giving out his call to the animals and strange creatures waiting to pounce on you? Most of these ideas are quite wrong! Many stories about jungles have been written by people who have never visited a real jungle.

This chapter is about the **tropical rain forest** but we shall use 'jungle' for short. We shall see that the jungle is full of life. There are many plants and animals living from ground level to the top of the highest trees. And the lives of all the plants and animals are intertwined in so many ways. The whole jungle, including the soil, rocks and the sun and rain is called an **ecosystem**. In an ecosystem, like the jungle, all the plants and animals play their part. If one living thing is disturbed many of the other living things are affected. *26 Life in the sea* describes how living things in the sea depend upon one another.

Plants of the jungle

Tropical rain forests grow near the equator. These jungles are hot (about 30°C), very humid and have no seasons. It is 'summer' all year round.

Look at Fig. 1 showing a profile (section) of a jungle. You can see four levels at which trees and plants grow.

Fig. 2 The sub-canopy layer in a rain forest

1 The canopy The leaves and branches of the tallest trees form the **canopy**. These trees are like huge umbrellas up to 50 metres tall. They collect energy from the sun for themselves but allow only a little of this energy to reach the plants below.

One of these trees is the *Shorea gibbosa* of Malaysia and Borneo. It grows to a height of 50 metres and a width of 5 metres. To help support its huge trunk, it grows special roots called **buttresses**.

2 The sub-canopy Below the canopy, in places where the sun shines through, small trees can grow. These form the **sub-canopy**.

3 The shrub layer In this layer there are young trees and shrubs. There is just enough light to enable them to grow.

4 The forest floor At ground level, where there is little light, there are ferns and seedlings. But deep inside a jungle it is so dark at ground level that very little can grow. Here on the forest floor are fallen leaves, branches, and dead animals. They are broken down by fungi and bacteria which are like 'workers' in a huge factory. The 'products' of this factory are chemicals called **nutrients** which help plants to grow.

Climbers and epiphytes

Two groups of plants do not easily fit into this profile of a jungle.

5 Climbers These plants use trees for support as they climb upwards in search of sunlight.

6 Epiphytes These are strange plants which may never touch the ground. They have roots which cling to tree trunks or branches for support and take water from hollows in trees.

Epiphytes do not obtain nutrients from the trees and so are *not* parasites.

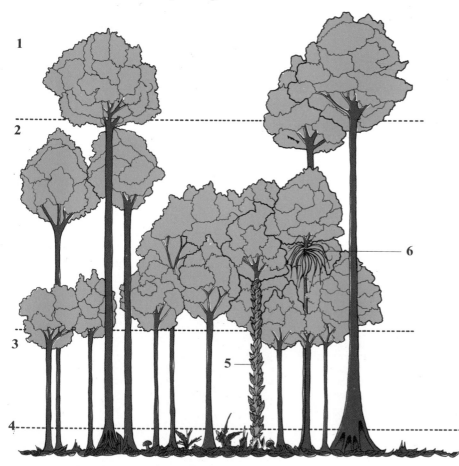

Fig. 1 Profile of a tropical rain forest

Animals of the jungle

Some jungles have elephants and leopards, and 'explorers' have to take great care! But most jungle animals move away at the slightest unusual noise.

Animals cannot make their own food so they have to eat plants or other animals. Plants are called **producers** because they can make food by **photosynthesis** using energy from sunlight. Animals are called **consumers** because they eat, or consume, plants or other animals. So animals depend upon plants in the jungle and other ecosystems.

Look at the **food chain** in the Fig. 3. The plant is eaten by a snail which is eaten by a bird such as a bulbul. This bird may then be eaten by a hawk. In the jungle, many of the food chains are linked together into a **food web**.

Fig. 3 A food chain

An ecosystem

The jungle is an ecosystem in which all the plants and animals play their part. But the Earth is also an ecosystem and we must take care that the jungles can always play their part.

Disturbing the jungle

If the food webs of a jungle are disturbed, many animals may suffer. In some countries, large areas of jungle have been destroyed to clear the ground for growing crops. Sadly, the nutrients in the soil, and often the soil itself, can be quickly washed away by heavy tropical rain leaving the ground barren. Even if the soil remains, it is poor in nutrients and they are no longer being replaced by decaying leaves and animals.

The jungles play an important role for the whole planet Earth. When photosynthesis occurs, carbon dioxide is absorbed from the air and oxygen is released. As more and more jungle is destroyed, so carbon dioxide will increase in the air. And remember too all the carbon dioxide which is released when coal and oil are burned to generate electricity. This increase in carbon dioxide may affect the world's weather.

QUESTIONS

1 What are epiphytes? How do they collect water?
2 Write out the animals in a food chain beginning with a leaf and ending with a snake. Use the food web to help.
3 Imagine that you live in a tropical country and that a large part of the jungle is to be cut down for timber. Write a letter to the owners of the land explaining why they should not destroy the jungle.
4 Write a reply to the letter of question 3 explaining why you as owners intend to go ahead with the plans.
5 Tropical rain forests and woodland in general are being destroyed at an ever-increasing rate. What will be the consequences to mankind if this is allowed to continue uncontrolled?

28 Feeding the world

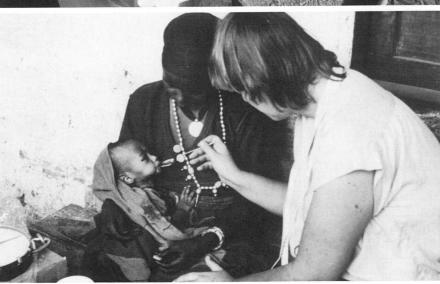

This chapter is about problems of feeding the world. Read these three passages and look at the photographs.

1 'No I didn't enjoy the meal at that restaurant. It must have had new owners since you visited it. . . . We had to wait ages before being served, and then the food they brought! There was a lot of it but my steak was overcooked. There was a good choice of vegetables and plenty to eat but they were nearly cold. I complained, of course, but I don't think I'll go there again.'

2 'We received our first food from the relief workers today. Food in the village had all gone and we had to walk 40 km to the relief centre. It took us three days. We were tired and hungry and our feet were swollen. But we were so pleased that our children had some rice to eat again.'

3 'It's just five years since I began working for Oxfam overseas. I have been on the edge of the Sahara desert now for eight months. The people back home are very generous in giving money to support us, but we don't have nearly enough food for these people. Their crops have failed for three years running and they have no money left to buy seed for sowing next year. All their money has been spent on buying food to survive. The world seems so unfair. I read about "butter mountains" and "grain mountains" in Europe. So much food is being produced that cannot be eaten, and yet I see thousands of people every day who are slowly starving to death.'

Fig. 1 More than enough to eat

Fig. 2 Basic food for a family

Fig. 3 An Oxfam worker

Some facts about food and hunger

1 More than 15 million people die a slow and lingering death from hunger each year.
2 500 million people in the world are severely malnourished and half of these are children.
3 Every day, the world produces about 1 kg of grain for every person on Earth. This is enough to provide adequate nourishment for everyone. Vast quantities of meat, fish, fruit and vegetables are also produced.

Why do millions die of hunger?

There are two main reasons why so many people die of hunger.

1 They are just not eating *enough* food and are starving. The energy in the food they eat is not sufficient to supply the body with the energy it needs to keep warm and to carry out all its functions.
2 The food being eaten does not contain all the *kinds* of food needed by the body to keep healthy. This problem is called **malnutrition**.

In some parts of the world, such as Ethiopia, many people suffer from both problems at the same time.

Malnutrition

To be healthy we need to eat protein, vitamins and minerals for growth of the body and repair of tissues. We also need to eat carbohydrates for growth and to give us energy. Sufficient food from each of the three groups below should be eaten regularly.

Group 1 Meat, fish, nuts, beans.
Group 2 Fresh fruit and vegetables.
Group 3 Cereals and cereal products, such as bread and rice.

Eating from each of these groups of foods gives a **balanced diet**. If people do not eat a balanced diet they may suffer from malnutrition.

Malnutrition is often caused by lack of sufficient **protein** in the diet. Protein is found in the foods in Group 1. More than 100 million children lack sufficient protein and suffer from a disease called **kwashiorkor**. This disease begins when infants are **weaned** from their mother's milk which is rich in protein. They then eat solid foods, such as rice, which are eaten by adults. These foods contain **carbohydrates** but very little protein. The children cannot cope with their new diet. They suffer from 'pot bellies' filled with fluid, weak limbs and thinning hair. They grow very slowly and have little energy. If their diet continues to lack the protein they need, they will die young.

Look at the table in Fig. 4 comparing typical daily diets of children in Britain with children in Africa and in the Caribbean. See how lucky children in Britain are [1].

Solving the world's food problems

Farmers and scientists produce enough food for everyone in the world. There is enough food of all the kinds required for everyone to be healthy. So why do some people starve whilst others are overweight? Why does Europe produce far more wheat, meat and dairy products than it needs? Why is this surplus food not sent to needy countries?

These questions are not questions for science. They are questions about *morals* and *opinions*. We have the ability to help if we choose to do so. One way of helping is to send surplus food to starving people. This is the least that we should do. But the best way to help is to provide the means for them to produce their own food.

1 Typical diet of British child aged 2		
Breakfast	15 g	cornflakes
	140 g	milk
	30 g	bread
	15 g	butter
	30 g	bacon
	60 g	tomato
Midmorning	140 g	orange juice
Dinner	60 g	stewed steak
	60 g	carrots
	60 g	potatoes
	140 g	milk ⎱ milk
	15 g	rice ⎰ pudding
Tea	60 g	scrambled egg
	60 g	bread
	120 g	apple
	20 g	butter
	15 g	jam
	140 g	milk
Bedtime	140 g	milk

Approx. analysis: 350 joules with 60 g of protein

2 Diet of an African girl aged 2		
Breakfast	36 g	millet flour
	14 g	leaves
	2 g	dawadawa*
	2 g	dry pepper
Lunch	18 g	millet flour
	2 g	shea butter
Supper	85 g	millet flour
	2 g	dawadawa*
	16 g	bean leaves
	2 g	dry pepper

Approx. analysis: 130 joules with 18·5 g protein

*fermented locust bean

3 Diet of a Caribbean boy aged 4		
Daily diet	3 g	cocoa
	72 g	white bread
	13 g	brown sugar
	20 g	margarine
	30 g	condensed milk

Approx. analysis: 130 joules with 8·7 g protein

Fig. 4 Daily diets in different parts of the world

QUESTIONS

1 What does *malnutrition* mean?
2 Look at the three diets in Fig. 4 and describe the main differences between them. Use the Groups of foods to help. What is missing from diets 2 and 3?
3 Write a letter to your MP, or arrange a class discussion, on the case for sending some of our surplus food to needy countries of Africa.

29 Diets around the world

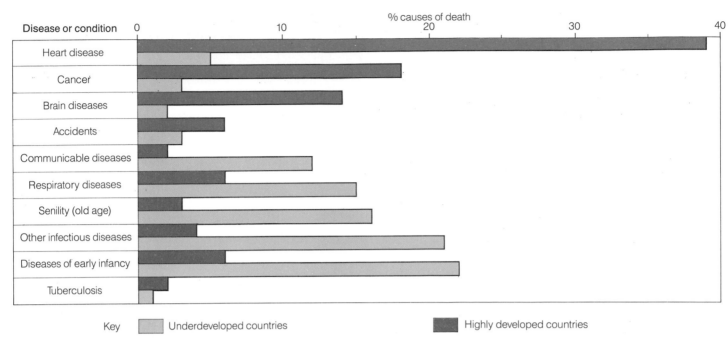

% causes of death

Disease or condition	
Heart disease	
Cancer	
Brain diseases	
Accidents	
Communicable diseases	
Respiratory diseases	
Senility (old age)	
Other infectious diseases	
Diseases of early infancy	
Tuberculosis	

Key ▢ Underdeveloped countries ■ Highly developed countries

Fig. 1 Percentage causes of death in developed and underdeveloped countries

Fig. 2 Useful information on a cereal packet

Eating habits vary throughout the world. What we eat has important effects on our health. This chapter describes some of the effects of our own diet on our health.

In India most people live on grain, dishes of rice and dahl and on wholemeal dough chapatis. Quite a lot of milk and cheese is used but often religious customs prevent the eating of meat. In China, milk products are not eaten. The staple diet is of rice and soya beans, with maize and bamboo shoots added occasionally. Favourite meats are pork, duck and chicken. Shellfish and fruit are also eaten. North Americans have a vast range of food available to them. Foods such as hot dogs and hamburgers are called 'fast foods' as they can be prepared and eaten very quickly.

In *28 Feeding the world* you can read about people who suffer from lack of food and unbalanced diets. Despite all the food available to us in the Western world, we too suffer from diseases and disorders thought to be due to our diet. For instance, over 13 million people in Britain have none of their original teeth due to too much sugar in their diet.

Fig. 1 is a bar chart showing the percentage causes of death in developed and underdeveloped countries. The high percentage of deaths from heart disease and cancer has been linked to the 'Western' diet. On the other hand, with good medical facilities and child care, the developed countries suffer far fewer deaths of young babies or from infectious diseases.

We require a lot of **fibre** in our diet and obtain most of it from the outside layers of grains (bran), vegetables and fruits. When we mill or peel the food we lose the fibre. Fibre absorbs water and increases the bulk of undigested food in our digestive system. This helps the gut muscles to push the food along quickly and so speeds up the elimination of waste from our bodies.

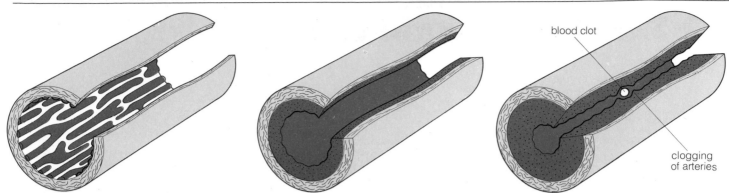

Fig. 3 Sections through an artery showing how fat deposits build up

Until the beginning of this century, all flour used in bread-making was made from whole wheat grains. This was because the millstones could not separate the grain from the bran. However, modern mills separate and discard the bran from the grain. They produce refined, low fibre flour. This has caused a big change in our diet by lowering the amount of fibre we eat. Recent research has clearly linked the lack of fibre in our diet with such ailments as diabetes, constipation, varicose veins, cancer of the bowel and heart disease.

People in less well developed countries, with a high fibre diet, suffer little from the diseases listed above. In the USA, certain religious groups have been found to suffer less from bowel cancer than the national average, due to their high fibre diets. The Seventh Day Adventists, for example, are mainly vegetarians, whilst the Mormons bake their own wholemeal bread.

The Japanese diet has become steadily Westernised over the last thirty years. This has brought some benefits and some problems. The overall balance of the diet has improved and increased the average weight of 15-year-olds by 3 kg per decade. But bowel cancer has increased because of reduced fibre intake.

Fat is important to use, supplying up to 42 per cent of our energy. It also helps the absorption of several important vitamins into the body. However a ten-year long study of 4000 American men has proved that a fatty diet increases the risk of a heart attack. Hard or 'saturated' fats such as butter, dripping and lard come from animals and contain **cholesterol**. Egg yolk is also rich in cholesterol. This is a waxy material that is deposited inside your arteries. It builds up over a number of years, makes the arteries narrower, and so restricts blood flow [Fig. 2]. If one of the arteries supplying the heart becomes blocked by a blood clot, the heart fails to get the oxygen it needs and a heart attack will occur.

Curiously enough, cholesterol is essential to us. It is an important part of cell membranes but our bodies make enough of it for their needs. So if we have a diet containing lots of cholesterol we just increase the level of it in our blood and therefore risk a heart attack. Fish, seeds, nuts and margarine are rich in soft, *polyunsaturated fats*. These actually *lower* the level of blood cholesterol. So you see, the amount of cholesterol our blood contains is greatly affected not just by the *amount* of fat we eat but also by the *type* of fat. This is why doctors and scientists now recommend us to eat less hard fat and replace it with soft fat.

Doctors suggest the following tips for a healthy lifestyle:

1 Eat less fat. Substitute low fat foods for high fat foods.
2 Eat more vegetables and cereals.
3 Cut down on sugar and salt.
4 Avoid excess alcohol.
5 Take regular exercise.
6 Do not smoke.

In Britain, laws have been passed to safeguard people who can only afford the cheaper foods. For instance, margarine and bread have vitamins and minerals added to them. Most flour, except wholemeal flour, is enriched with calcium in the form of calcium carbonate. The next time you are at the breakfast table, read the list of ingredients on the side of the cereal packet. You will be surprised at how many nutrients you consume from a bowl of cereal.

QUESTIONS

1 Why do you think that infectious diseases are more common in undeveloped countries, and cancer is more common in developed countries?
2 Make a list of what you have eaten on one particular day. Work out how much fibre and fat you may have consumed.
3 Why does fibre help the passage of food along the alimentary canal?
4 How good for you are the popular 'fast foods'?
5 Why do you think the incidence of bowel cancer has increased in Japan? How could this disease be prevented?

30 Saving the world's children

Amarun and Tahir

Amarun Begum lives in a remote village in Bangladesh. The village has no piped fresh water and food is always scarce. Last year Amarun lost her two-year-old daughter, Mina. Mina died of diarrhoea and malnutrition. **Diarrhoea** is a symptom of diseases which cause faeces to be very fluid and to pass through the body very quickly. **Malnutrition** is caused by important foods being missed from a diet and is common in very poor countries.

Now it looked as if Amarun would lose Hasan, her one-year-old son, in the same way.

The sanitation and hygiene in the village were very poor and allowed germs to spread very easily [Fig. 1]. Amarun tried her best to keep Hasan healthy but, just like Mina last year, Hasan was now suffering with diarrhoea. For several days the poor child had suffered many attacks. Fluids, salt and other minerals vital to his precious life had been pouring out of his body. Amarun feared the worst.

Amarun, like other mothers in the village, tried the only thing she knew to help Hasan. She starved him to 'rest his bowel'. Sadly, this caused Hasan to become even more undernourished and the attacks of diarrhoea came more often.

Fortunately for Amarun and Hasan, just when things looked really hopeless a Village Health Volunteer (VHV), called Tahir, visited their village. Tahir came to look at Hasan. Amarun was surprised at the simple remedy she was given. She had to feed Hasan on something he called Oral Rehydration Salts (ORS, see Fig. 2). Tahir just showed her how to dissolve powder from a packet in drinking water.

Then Tahir showed her how to make up her own ORS. Tahir gave Amarun a special spoon [Fig. 3] to measure the correct quantities of salt and sugar to be dissolved in Hasan's drinking water. He explained that she should use the smaller scoop at one end of the spoon to add one level scoop of salt to one litre of water. Tahir asked Amarun to taste the water. She found it slightly salty like the taste of her own tears. Next Tahir told her to use the larger scoop at the other end of the spoon to add eight level scoops of sugar to the salty water and to mix it in well. And that was all there was to it!

Amarun was amazed that such a cheap and simple remedy could cure Hasan. Even if she forgot what she had to do, the instructions were printed on the spoon handle in her own native language.

Amarun followed Tahir's instructions closely for several weeks. Sure enough, Hasan recovered well and began to eat normal food. With encouragement from Tahir, Amarun paid regular visits to the newly opened Health Station in her village. Here she was helped to choose the best local foods to give Hasan. Tahir also told Amarun and her friends of several other simple things they could do to help them all lead healthier lives.

Fig. 1 A breeding ground for diarrhoea: waste water is in contact with water used for drinking and washing

Fig. 2 Oral rehydration mixture recommended by the World Health Organisation (WHO)

3·50 g	sodium chloride
2·50 g	sodium hydrogencarbonate
1·50 g	potassium chloride
20·00 g	glucose
	or
40·00 g	sucrose (whichever is cheaper or more readily available)
1·00 l	drinking water

Fig. 3 A specially designed spoon for measuring Oral Rehydration Salts. Instructions in local languages are printed on each spoon

Help from UNICEF

UNICEF stands for the United Nations International Childrens' Emergency Fund. People working for UNICEF have publicised four simple plans to help in saving children in developing countries. The plans are so simple that most parents can follow them. And the things needed for the plans are so cheap that even the poorest countries can afford them.

1 Growth charts
2 Oral rehydration
3 Breast feeding
4 Immunisation

You can now read about each plan in turn.

Growth charts

A growth chart costing just 7p is used for each child [Fig. 4]. A child's weight is recorded on its chart every month and a curve is drawn to show the variation in weight. The weight curve should rise steadily. If a child's weight follows the curve for a healthy child, all is well. If the weight curve becomes 'flat', it usually means that the child needs more food. If the weight curve begins to fall, it gives a warning that better nutrition and, probably, medical care are needed.

Children are weighed every month at a weighing station and a growth chart is marked. Weighing stations are found at popular spots in towns and villages such as the market place. If a problem is spotted, a Village Health Volunteer like Tahir is around to give advice.

Oral rehydration

Oral rehydration is the remedy used for Hasan in the story above. The cost is about £1 per child per year. In the last few years, more than 90 countries have begun to develop national plans for the control of diseases in the diarrhoea family.

Breast feeding

A healthy mother will normally give birth to a healthy baby of satisfactory weight. But for the next six months, the baby needs to be fed with milk. Breast milk gives the correct substances for the baby's normal growth. Breast milk also contains **antibodies** which are special chemicals passed to the baby to give natural protection against infections. So UNICEF is encouraging mothers to breast feed their babies. Breast feeding costs nothing and may save up to £100 often spent on buying milk or milk powder.

Immunisation

It costs about £3 to vaccinate a child against the killer diseases of diphtheria, tetanus, whooping cough, poliomyelitis, measles and tuberculosis (TB). This is not a high price to pay for protection for life against these diseases, is it?

UNICEF and the World Health Organisation (WHO) have devised 'cold chains' to transport vaccine. The vaccine is carried in refrigerated packs by horses, camels, jeep or whatever transport is available. It is hoped that all the world's 500 million children under the age of five can be vaccinated by 1990.

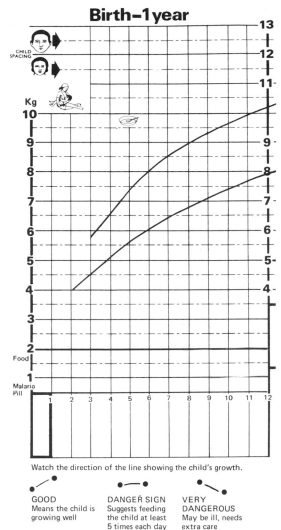

Birth–1 year

Watch the direction of the line showing the child's growth.

GOOD
Means the child is growing well

DANGER SIGN
Suggests feeding the child at least 5 times each day

VERY DANGEROUS
May be ill, needs extra care

Encourage mother to give extra food more often to help her child to grow.

Fig. 4 WHO growth chart

QUESTIONS

1 Why is diarrhoea so dangerous in growing children?
2 Why does diarrhoea spread so easily in poor communities?
3 Write down the remedy for diarrhoea given by Tahir. Explain why you think that the two substances to be dissolved help to cure diarrhoea.
4 Explain why growth charts help in the care of babies?
5 Why does UNICEF try to persuade mothers to feed their babies on breast milk rather than on milk powder?

Index